CONTENTS

ABOUT THIS BOOK

This *Step by Step Guide* has been produced by the editors of Insight Guides, whose books have set the standard for visual travel guides since 1970. With top-quality photography and authoritative recommendations, this guidebook brings you the very best of Berlin in a series of 14 tailor-made tours.

WALKS AND TOURS

The tours in the book provide something to suit all budgets, tastes and trip lengths. As well as covering Berlin's many classic attractions, the routes track lesser-known sights and up-and-coming areas; there is also an excursion to the palaces at Potsdam for those who want to extend their visit outside the city.

The tours embrace a range of interests, so whether you are an art or architecture fan, a gourmet, a lover of flora, a history buff or have kids to entertain, you will find an option to suit.

We recommend that you read the whole of a tour before setting out. This should help you to familiarise yourself with the route and enable you to plan where to stop for refreshments – options for this are shown in the 'Food

Above: East Berlin memorabilia at Mondos Arts; East Side Gallery *(see p.89)*; dome at the Reichstag *(see p.42)*; Filmmuseum; Buddy Bears *(see p.19)*.

and Drink' boxes, recognisable by the knife-and-fork sign, on most pages within the tours.

For our pick of the walks by theme, consult Recommended Tours For… *(see p.6–7)*.

OVERVIEW

The tours are set in context by this introductory section, giving an overview of the city to set the scene, plus background information on food and drink, shopping and entertainment. A succinct history timeline highlights the key events that have shaped Berlin over the centuries.

DIRECTORY

Also supporting the tours is a Directory chapter, comprising a user-friendly, clearly organised A–Z of practical information, our pick of where to stay while you are in the city and select restaurant listings; these eateries complement the more low-key cafés and restaurants that feature within the tours and are intended to offer a wider choice for evening dining. Also included are nightlife listings, reflecting Berlin's growing status as a major arts and clubbing capital.

The Author

Jürgen Scheunemann has lived in Berlin since 1987. After studying at the city's Freie Universität, he wrote for Berlin's listings magazine *tip* and the leading daily newspaper, *Der Tagesspiegel*. As a historian, Jürgen is particularly interested in the city's history and its ongoing evolution. His experience of life in Berlin and his fascination with the city's social and cultural scenes have found expression in several travel guides, as well as historical and coffee-table books. Jürgen currently lives in Charlottenburg, his favourite district.

Margin Tips

Shopping tips, historical facts, handy hints and information on activities help visitors to make the most of their time in Berlin.

Feature Boxes

Notable topics are highlighted in these special boxes.

Key Facts Box

This box gives details of the distance covered on the tour, plus an estimate of how long it should take. It also states where the route starts and finishes, and gives key travel information such as which days are best to do the route or handy transport tips.

Route Map

Detailed cartography shows the tour clearly plotted with numbered dots. Note that the ß in 'Straße' (street) appears as 'ss' throughout the book ('Strasse'), although as ß on the maps. For even more detailed mapping, see the pull-out map that is slotted inside the back cover.

Food and Drink

Recommendations of where to stop for refreshment are given in these boxes. The numbers prior to each restaurant/café name link to references in the main text. Restaurants in the Food and Drink boxes are plotted on city maps.

The € signs at the end of each entry reflect the approximate cost of a two-course meal for one, with a glass of house wine. These should be seen as a guide only. Price ranges, also quoted on the inside back flap for easy reference, are:

€€€€	60 euros and above
€€€	40–60 euros
€€	25–40 euros
€	25 euros and below

Footers

Look here for the tour name, a map reference and the main attraction on the double page.

ARCHITECTURE FANS

Explore the Sony Center and the other new glass-and-steel buildings around Potsdamer Platz (walk 4) and indulge in the great historic landmarks along the boulevard Unter den Linden (walk 6) or on the Gendarmenmarkt (walk 9).

RECOMMENDED TOURS FOR...

ART AND MUSEUM BUFFS

Top arty tours are the Unesco-protected Museum Island, home to five internationally important museums (walk 7), and an afternoon in the art galleries around the Kulturforum in the Tiergarten district (walk 4).

CLUBBERS

Spend a long night in Mitte's vibrant Scheunenviertel (walk 8) with its pubs, bars and clubs, before heading to the more alternative Kreuzberg (walk 11) or the adjoining Friedrichshain (walk 13).

COLD WAR AND WALL CONNECTIONS

Dive into Cold War history at Checkpoint Charlie and the adjacent museum on the Berlin Wall (walk 10). Away from the tourist crowds, trace the Wall back to the East Side Gallery (walk 13).

FAMILIES WITH KIDS

See Berlin on a bus on tour 1, or spend time at the Berlin zoo and aquarium, followed by a stroll in the Tiergarten (walk 3).

FOODIES

Good restaurants can be found across the city, but a great selection is clustered in the Scheunenviertel area (walk 8) or in the bohemian Prenzlauer Berg (tour 12). Time permitting, spend the later part of the night checking out restaurants in Kreuzberg and Schöneberg (walk 11).

PRUSSIAN PALACES

Take time out to visit Frederick the Great's palace and park of Sanssouci at Potsdam (tour 14). This is an easy day trip (accessible by public transport) from central Berlin.

RAINY DAYS

Take refuge in the Sony Center and the museums and galleries of the Kulturforum (walk 4), or in the world-class museums on Museum Island (walk 7). Learn more about the city's history at the Story of Berlin on Ku'damm (walk 2). Alternatively, see the sights from the shelter of a public bus, on our highlights trip (tour 1).

SHOPPERS

Take a stroll down the Ku'damm in Charlottenburg and pay a visit to the continent's largest department store, the KaDeWe (walk 2). Head over to what was East Berlin and inspect the luxury shops of the Friedrichstadtpassagen (walk 9) before diving into the hip fashion scene in the Scheunenviertel (walk 8).

WORLD WAR II REMEMBRANCE

Explore the area around the Brandenburg Gate and Wilhelmstrasse, the old centre of power and the former location of Hitler's so-called Führerbunker (walk 5). Reflect on the war at the Holocaust Memorial on the same tour, or at the equally moving Gedenkstätte Deutscher Widerstand, at the end of walk 4.

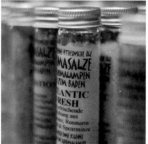

OVERVIEW

An overview of Berlin's geography, customs and culture, plus illuminating background information on food and drink, shopping, entertainment and nightlife, and history.

INTRODUCTION

Berlin represents the triumphs and tragedies of European history as no other city on the continent. It is, moreover, a city that publicly acknowledges its past – good and bad – with museums, memorials and historic buildings.

Berlin is located in the far east of Germany, approximately 80km (50 miles) away from the Polish border and some 150km (93 miles) from the Baltic coast. It is situated within a typical North European flatland (Berlin's highest mountain, the Grosser Müggelberg, measures a mere 115m/377ft), with dry soil, not very fertile land and only a few rivers. Berlin is at the confluence of two of these rivers, the Spree and the Havel.

By any standard, the city-state of Berlin (one of 16 German states) is laid out on a vast scale. It covers a total of 892 sq km (344 sq m), with a north–south length of 38km (24 miles) and a breadth, east to west, of 45km (28 miles). The state comprises 12 districts or boroughs, the borders of which generally relate to the historic evolution of the region. Despite its size, Berlin is easy to navigate – thanks to its modern highway network and extensive public transport system.

Above: reminders of the city's Jewish history at the Jewish Museum; a Trabant.

CITY DISTRICTS

Visitors to Berlin who knew the city 20 years ago would no doubt be astounded by the shifts in the personalities of the various *Bezirke* (boroughs). The centre of the city is Mitte, where the major cultural institutions are located. The Tiergarten district, with its leafy park of the same name, is to Mitte's west and leads to Charlottenburg, which is upscale, if less prominent, since the fall of the Wall. South of the centre is Kreuzberg, home to many of the newer landmarks and a neighbourhood legendary for its alternative youth culture and large Turkish population. Schöneberg is located just west and is more gentrified, with a prominent gay scene. Meanwhile, the northern district Prenzlauer Berg has transformed from a poor district into a trendy hub with a thriving café culture and stylish boutiques.

EAST AND WEST

When Berlin was divided up at the end of World War II, it was appropriate that the Soviet sector, devoted to the Communist experiment, should take in a large number of the working-class areas, while West Berlin had at its centre the eminently bourgeois neighbourhood of Charlottenburg. After the total destruction wrought by World War II, the eastern sector was hastily

rebuilt in uninspired Socialist style, while the West was regenerated with tasteless 'Wirtschaftswunder' buildings.

On reunification, two sets of people psychologically attuned to different economic and social systems were thrust together, and unforeseen problems emerged. As tens of thousands of East Germans came to settle in the West, entitling them to 'adjustment' money, housing subsidies and job retraining from the Bonn government, the financial burden of reunification began to trouble West Germans, while a small minority of disgruntled West Berliners even began to wish that the Wall had never been knocked down.

For many of the inhabitants of East Berlin, too, the merger with the West was less than perfect. The sud-

Above from far left: the Quadriga statue, on the Brandenburg Gate; Frederick the Great's Prussian sunburst, at Sans-souci; 1987 *Berlin* memorial, on Tauentzienstrasse; Gothic-style street sign on Maassenstrasse.

Left: the Holocaust Memorial.

Ostalgie

As the film *Goodbye Lenin!* (2003) illustrates, there are some East Germans for whom reunification must have proved simply too much of a shock. Others have accepted the passing of the GDR, but retain a nostalgia (hence the term *Ostalgie*) for the old certainties of jobs for life and workplace kindergartens. Basic items such as food and household products from the GDR are also fondly remembered, and some 'Ostprodukte' (Eastern Products) are now objects of retro fashion.

den impact of the West's free-market economic system was in some cases disastrous, with people losing such previously enjoyed benefits as controlled rents and job security *(see margin left)*.

CULTURAL RENEWAL

What is undeniable, however, is that the collapse of the Wall and the integration of two independent cities have created a wealth and diversity of culture. With no fewer than three opera houses, three major symphony orchestras and two national art galleries, the status of Berlin as the united Germany's artistic capital is beyond doubt.

Since then, in addition, the Kulturforum in the Tiergarten district has been expanded, the magnificent Museumsinsel in the middle of the River Spree is undergoing restoration, and major museums such as the Jüdisches Museum have opened their doors. Western Berlin's Schaubühne, along with the Berliner Ensemble, Volksbühne and Deutsches Theater from the East, now make up one of the world's most formidable theatre establishments, promoting both the classical tradition and the avant-garde. With the Berlin Film Festival as its flagship, German cinema is also regaining the excitement of its great creative period in the 1920s, a time commemorated in the Filmmuseum Berlin *(see p.46)*.

CLIMATE

Visitors frequently find that Berlin's generally mild climate exceeds its reputation. Although northeastern Germany in general experiences lower temperatures than the west of the country, spring is often surprisingly warm, and in summer the city really flourishes. The metropolis's built-up area also creates its own microclimate, as the city's buildings store up heat. Temperatures can therefore be up to 4°C (7.2°F) higher in the city than in the surrounding countryside.

In summer, temperatures often reach 22–25°C (in the 70s°F) and rarely dip below 12°C (54°F). Winters are cold, with temperatures generally in the range of -2°C to 4°C (upper 20s to upper 30s°F). Annual rainfall averages 571mm (22½ inches), and snowfall is generally moderate, occuring between December and March.

POPULATION

Berlin is by far the largest city in Germany. The city itself has a population of roughly 3.4 million people, while the wider metropolitan area of Berlin-Brandenburg has a total population of some 4.4 million.

Historically, the city has always attracted immigrants. French Huguenots arrived in the 17th century, Jewish people in the 19th century and a significant influx of Turkish 'Gastarbeiter'

(guest workers) in the 1960s. The city remains a cosmopolitan one even today, with 14 percent (almost 500,000 people) being of non-German origin. Of these, the largest constituent is the Turkish population, numbering some 120,000, and forming the largest Turkish community outside Turkey.

In recent history, both East and West Berlin have had 'older' populations on average than most other international cities of comparable size. This trend has, however, reversed considerably since the fall of the Berlin Wall. As younger Berlin's 'alternative scene' has gained momentum, it has revived the reputation the city had in the 1920s for lively and wildly independent-minded creativity.

ECONOMY

Economically, Berlin has long been an almost bankrupt city. During the period when the city was divided between East and West, the governments of each side provided huge subsidies to bolster their political power-bases. Since reunification, however, the subsidies have dwindled.

Despite the development of cultural, tourism, services and high-tech sectors, local industry and commerce have proved inadequate to the task of making up the shortfall. For historical reasons, top international companies have made their headquarters elsewhere, as has Germany's important banking and insurance industry. Consequently, a Berlin mayor's quip that the city is 'poor but sexy' remains a sad truth, and unemployment rates remain as high as 13 percent.

GREEN SPACES

Despite its stone, steel and glass, Berlin is the greenest metropolis in Europe, with almost 40 percent of its area covered by lakes and rivers, parkland and woods. Besides the Tiergarten and the River Spree in the city centre, the southwest suburbs have the forest of the Grunewald, the River Havel and the Wannsee, while the north has the Tegel forest and lake. Small garden colonies abound, with flourishing farming communities, such as Lübars, set inside the city boundaries. To all of this, eastern Berlin adds its own Grosser Müggelsee as well as the woods and parkland around Treptow and Köpenick.

There are more delightful excursions to be had beyond the city limits. Potsdam, at the other end of the Glienicke Bridge, lies within easy reach for a visit to Frederick the Great's Sanssouci Palace, with its extensive grounds; or you could go walking in the surrounding forests and parks of Charlottenhof, Petzow and Werder; try a spot of boating on the Templiner Lake; or even make a pilgrimage to the monastery of Lehnin near Brandenburg.

Above from far left: the Alte National-galerie, illuminated by night; Berlin subway.

Local Dialect
Authentic Berliners speak a fast-paced dialect sounding even harsher and more scratchy than ordinary German. Many 'ch' sounds are replaced by 'ck', such as in 'Icke' (meaning 'I') instead of the High German 'ich', for example. An 'auf' ('on') becomes an 'uff', while the 'ein' becomes an 'een' and so forth. Nicknamed the 'Berliner Schnauze' (Berlin gob), the dialect is also associated with wit and a down-to-earth attitude.

FOOD AND DRINK

There's more to Berlin's restaurant and bar scene than just beer and sausages. As a multicultural city, it offers a wide variety of world cuisines as well as a range of local specialities, all at surprisingly affordable prices.

LOCAL CUISINE

Berlin's local food is renowned neither for its refined recipes nor its elegant style, but it certainly is tasty, filling and hearty. Historically, Berlin has been a working-class city, whose population needed sustenance at an affordable price. Similarly, the rural population of the surrounding region of Brandenburg demanded a simple yet nutritious style of food.

Today, regional cuisine has made a huge comeback, as young chefs are re-inventing traditional recipes. Their art has reclaimed local dishes hitherto encountered only in sub-standard versions in some of the city's pubs. Fresh produce such as fish, game and locally grown vegetables, reliance only on what is in season, and the forgoing of exotic ingredients characterise this new, back-to-basics cuisine. Restaurants such as Hartmanns, E.T.A. Hoffmann, Altes Zollhaus and even the Michelin-starred Facil are celebrating this trend.

Typical local dishes include Eisbein (pork knuckle) with sauerkraut, Kasseler (dried and salted pork meat) with sauerkraut, pan-fried liver (veal or pork) with apples, mashed potatoes and fried onions, Brandenburg duck with red and green cabbage and salted potatoes and – one of the very few lighter dishes – fried pike-perch.

Pubs often offer variations of these dishes – usually in smaller portions. Their traditional fare includes various kinds of sausages *(see margin, left)*, 'Bulette' (a fried burger, usually served cold with spicy mustard), cucumbers and other pickled vegetables, and several types of cheese.

A visit to Berlin would not be complete without checking out the local bakeries and pastry places. Berliners love bread loaves and rolls and have a huge selection of local varieties, often with names that sound peculiar even to Germans: a 'Schrippe', for example, is a regular, crispy white roll, whereas a 'Schusterjunge' (literally a 'club line') is a hard rye roll. A 'Pfannkuchen' in Berlin is not (as in the rest of Germany) a pancake, but a fluffy doughnut filled with jelly.

HIGH-END RESTAURANTS

The upper crust of European gourmets has always looked down on greasy

Currywurst

The archetypical Berlin sausage is a local post-World War II invention, created by Hertha Heuwer in 1949 in Charlottenburg (the house at the corner of Kantstrasse- and Kaiser-Friedrich-Strasse bears a commemorative plaque). Heuwer made her sausage from the simple ingredients available at the time: boiled pork sausage, curry powder, tomato and Worcestershire sauce. Today, the city's better Imbisse (kiosks or booths), such as Ku'damm 195, offer Currywurst 'mit or ohne Darm' (with or without intestinal skin) and the fries 'rot' (with tomato ketchup) or 'rot-weiss' (with tomato ketchup and mayonnaise).

Berlin kitchens. Indeed, owing to the division of the city, West Berlin had only a few high-class chefs and hardly any Michelin stars, while haute cuisine was almost unheard of in Socialist East Berlin. All of this changed when the Wall came down. In moved the international hotel chains capable of supporting top-rank chefs, who often had a curiosity about long-forgotten regional recipes.

The late 1990s brought a slight decline in the fashion for high dining, but since then a new generation of young chefs has revitalised the scene, making Berlin the city with the highest number of Michelin stars in Germany. Many of these establishments are also remarkably affordable.

PUBS (KNEIPEN)

'Kneipen' are a speciality of Berlin. Typically, they are down-to-earth, no-nonsense pubs, offering beer on tap, hard liquor (but rarely cocktails), a small wine selection and hearty traditional German cooking with a regional accent. There are an estimated 6,000 of them in Berlin, and their variety is impressive. Most are frequented only by residents of the neighbourhood in which they are situated, making each pub as individual as the street corner on which it is found. Initially, invading the regulars' hallowed locale may seem intimidating, but even the grumpiest of Berliners usually loosens up after a couple of beers.

Above from far left: haute cuisine – a reflection of the city's burgeoning food scene; a welcoming beer; apple strudel; enjoying a classic sausage sandwich.

Above and left: coffee and continental breakfast; Bratwurst roll with sauerkraut.

ETHNIC VARIETY

Above: tempting caramel and cream sweets; fresh rhubarb at Kreuzberg's Turkish Market.

There is probably no other city in Germany that offers the same variety of ethnic cuisines as Berlin. Over its history, the city has welcomed wave after wave of immigrants, each bringing with it its own cuisine. In the past few decades, Turkish and Middle Eastern influences have had the greatest effect on the city's food culture. In addition to the ubiquitous Döner Kebab 'Imbisse', there is now also a new generation of more upmarket Turkish restaurants, such as Defne.

Asian food has also experienced huge growth in popularity in Berlin in recent years. Avoid the many inexpensive, low-quality neighbourhood Chinese joints, and head instead for the more refined Vietnamese, Malaysian, Japanese, Thai and cross-over restaurants such as Shiro i Shiro, Monsieur Vuong, Pan Asia, Kuchi or Zing *(see p.114–17)*.

Other national cuisines that have made their presence felt in Berlin include those from Italy, Spain and Greece. In addition, there are a number of Russian and Eastern European restaurants, with some of latter specialising in traditional Jewish cooking. In contrast with some other European capitals, however, there are relatively few African or Caribbean restaurants, or good Indian eateries.

CHAINS

Germany has only a few domestic restaurant chains. One of the more popular is Wienerwald, selling crispy, slowly roasted half-chickens. A more upmarket chain, albeit one with few outlets in Berlin, is Mövenpick. Local 'chains' within Berlin include Hasir, for Turkish food, and the Maximilian Currywurst takeaways. Healthier choices include Nordsee – for fresh fish – and Soup Culture.

WHERE TO EAT

Berlin offers a wide variety of places to eat, from the simple and affordable to the elegant and expensive. The cheapest places to satisfy your hunger are at 'Imbisse' – German or Turkish (and sometimes Asian) booths found on almost every corner of the city. German Imbisse mostly sell sausages such as the Currywurst, while Turkish ones sell Döner Kebab. While the quality of the food is generally what you might expect, some of the sausage stalls can be surprisingly good.

German Wines

The most highly regarded German wines are those of the Rheingau. Among the labels to look for are Schloss Johannis-berger, Hattenheimer, Kloster Eberbacher, Steinberger and Rüdesheimer. The best of the Rhine Valley red wines come from Assmannshausen and Ingelheim. From Rheinhessen, try the Niersteiner Domtal and Oppenheimer. Delicate Mosel wines include Bernkasteler, Piesporter and Graacher.

An alternative for a quick bite are Berlin's many bakeries, many of which sell 'belegte Brötchen' (sandwiches) as well as coffee and cakes or pastries. Coffeehouses have been popular in Berlin long before Starbucks, and two excellent local chains are Einstein and Café Balzac. In addition, some cafés serve full meals or bistro fare as well as the traditional German 'Kaffee und Kuchen' (Coffee and Cake) in the afternoon.

While Imbisse, Kneipen, cafés and chains can be found anywhere in Berlin, for international cuisine you should head over to the districts of Charlottenburg and Wilmersdorf, particularly around the Ku'damm and Savignyplatz. High-end restaurants, including many Michelin-starred ones, are often located in luxury hotels, but there are also several independent establishments.

A younger and hipper crowd is drawn to Mitte's Scheunenviertel, or to Kreuzberg with its concentration of ethnic eateries. Here and in neighbouring Schöneberg, as well as in parts of Friedrichshain, you will find the city's funkiest bars and restaurants. Many of the places you will come across in these districts are 'Szenerestaurants' – often hip or alternative pubs, cafés or bars that also serve food. Meanwhile, Prenzlauer Berg offers a mixture of all types of establishment, while the Tiergarten district (including Potsdamer Platz) offers only a few notable eating destinations.

Another inexpensive but fun way to sample local cuisine is to visit one of the city's market halls (such as Kreuzberg's Marheinke-Markthalle). Most open on Wednesdays and Saturdays, and enable you to try a wide range of fresh local produce.

DRINKS

Berlin has its fair share of beer brands, but does not come close to the celebrated beer cultures of Munich or Cologne. Even if they are no match for West German and Bavarian beers, the local brews – such as Schultheiss, Berliner Kindl and Berliner Pilsener – are nonetheless popular, particularly if they are fresh 'vom Fass' (on tap).

A Berlin speciality is 'Berliner Weisse mit Schuss', a light wheatbased beer with a shot of woodruff juice, turning the drink green. 'Molle mit Korn', a beer with schnapps, is also still widely enjoyed in local pubs.

Schnapps are traditionally distilled from cherries (Kirschwasser), plums (Zwetschgenwasser) or raspberries (Himbeergeist). In addition, German brandy (Weinbrand) is popular.

In addition, there is also a wide range of fine German wines to choose from – Berlin's top restaurants have some of the country's largest wine cellars. Berliners also love to drink cocktails, particularly in the city's many riverbeach and rooftop lounges. While there are no special Berlin cocktails, each bar has its own way of mixing international classics.

Table Manners
On one or two of the long tables in pubs (Kneipen) or larger restaurants, you will occasionally see a sign proclaiming 'Stammtisch,' which means a table for regulars; the custom dates back to the medieval craft guilds. It is otherwise standard practice for strangers to sit together, usually after a polite inquiry as to whether one of the empty places is 'frei' (free). As they sit down they wish each other 'Mahlzeit' or 'Guten Appetit'.

SHOPPING

Go shopping in Berlin, and you'll end up with a motley collection of trophies in your suitcase as you return through customs. Shoppers are particularly spoilt for choice in designer and alternative fashions, antiques, porcelain and books.

SHOPPING AREAS

Berlin is spread out over such a large area that shoppers will need to pick the destination for their afternoon's retail therapy very carefully. A priority might be to seek out concentrations of one-off boutiques, since many of the large chain stores have branches in several of the city's major districts.

Above: books, shoes and children's mobile – just some of the plethora of goods for sale in Berlin.

West Berlin
Berlin's main shopping area is still the Kurfürstendamm. The further west you go along the avenue, the more upmarket the shops become, while towards the eastern end you'll find mostly chains and budget stores. Nearby, on Tauentzienstrasse, is the city's largest department store, Kaufhaus des Westens (KaDeWe for short).

The side streets off the Ku'damm also harbour some interesting retail opportunities, from antiquarian booksellers to fashion boutiques. Particularly worth seeking out are Bleibtreu-, Uhland-, Schlüter- and Knesebeckstrasse, as well as the area around Savignyplatz and nearby Mommsenstrasse. Quirky, budget German, Turkish and Eastern European stores can be found a few steps away, along Kantstrasse, while the Wilmersdorfer Strasse is Berlin's largest pedestrian zone, and accommodates affordable chain outlets.

East Berlin
In East Berlin, Friedrichstrasse (and the Friedrichstadtpassagen) offers the main competition to Ku'damm in the West. Particular destinations here include Galeries Lafayette and the smart Department Store 206.

Otherwise, the area around Hackescher Markt in Mitte's Scheunenviertel is worth visiting for its concentration of hip fashion-brand stores. There is also a smattering of independents here, offering their own unique fashion designs.

The district of Kreuzberg is the place to go for alternative fashion, with many of its most appealing stores clustered around Bergmannstrasse and Oranienstrasse. Neighbouring Friedrichshain is less promising territory for shoppers.

Shopping Malls
If you want to visit a shopping mall, the best are the Potsdamer Platz Arkaden in Tiergarten and the Alexa complex in Mitte. Southern Berlin

also has some smaller shopping malls, along Schlossstrasse and Hauptstrasse.

WHAT TO BUY

Berlin is particularly fertile territory for antiques hunters, bookworms, record aficionados and art buffs as well as fashion victims. Antiques, old books, records and second-hand clothes are relatively affordable in Berlin. By contrast, branded fashion – even German labels such as Boss, Joop, Jil Sander, Adidas or Puma – is quite expensive.

If you are looking for souvenirs, consider the high-quality porcelain made by the Königliche Porzellan Manufaktur (KPM). It specialises in replicas of the exhibits found in the state museums on Museum Island. If your taste is for something less conventional, you can buy Russian and East German uniforms or even pieces of the Wall from street vendors. Most of these, though, are in fact Chinese- or Eastern European-manufactured fakes. Visitors are on safer ground, however, with KaDeWe-branded products, as well as 'Buddy Bears' – coloured, painted decorative bears sold on many street corners.

SALES

In the past, German clothing and department stores were allowed to hold two annual sales, the 'Sommer-schlussverkauf' and the 'Winterschluss-verkauf', usually held in late August and late January. Thanks to the liberalisation of consumer laws, this has now changed, and many shops hold sales at various times throughout the year. In addition, summer and winter sales tend to start increasingly early (mid-January and early August) and last ever longer.

If you are a non-EU citizen, note that you will be able to claim back the VAT (Mehrwertsteuer, or MwSt), which at 19 percent on most products is high. It's only worth the bother over a certain amount; ask for a Tax-Free Shopping Cheque for the amount to be refunded and keep this to hand in at the airport when you leave.

OPENING TIMES

Changes in consumer laws in Germany have also enabled shops to open for longer. Most larger stores and shops in central locations are open Monday to Friday from 9 or 10am until 8pm, and on Saturday until 6 or 8pm. Family-run businesses tend to close at 6pm on weekdays and at 2 or 4pm on Saturdays. Large department stores, such as KaDeWe often have their own late-opening hours on Fridays.

Seasonal variations include Sunday opening in the central shopping areas on the four weekends before Christmas. There is also a biannual 'Lange Nacht' (last weekend in March and October; www.lange-nacht-des-shoppings.de), when shops along the Ku'damm stay open until midnight.

Above from far left: rifling through vinyl – Berlin has good bargains for record aficionados; pretty bath products at Belladonna on Bergmannstrasse. Kreuzberg; Ute Hentschel fashions; sign for the city's largest department store, the Kaufhaus des Westens.

Flea and Antiques Markets
One of Berlin's best markets for antiques is the 'Antik- und Kunstmarkt' in Strasse des 17 Juni (Sat and Sun 10am–6pm). While prices are high, haggling is encouraged. A 'Kunst- und Nostalgiemarkt' around Museum Island (Sat and Sun 2–9pm) is a somewhat smaller affair, but also worth a visit.

ENTERTAINMENT

Whether your taste is for opera or techno, string quartets or hard rock, classical theatre or underground cinema, Berlin will not only offer it, but, more than likely, excel in it.

Berlin offers a peculiar mixture of high and low art, state-run and independent venues, and conservative and anything-goes cultures. From the wilder dance clubs of Kreuzberg to the classical discipline of the Berlin Philharmonic, there is certainly no lack of choice.

THEATRE

Berlin has been at the heart of German-language theatre since the 1920s. Many productions are only suitable for those with an excellent understanding of German, but there are also musical and variety shows that should appeal to all. One venue that caters specifically to English-speaking audiences, however, is the Kreuzberg-based English Theatre (tel: 030-693 5692; www.etberlin.de; *see p.118*).

Among the most important German-language theatres is the Schaubühne (Kurfürstendamm 153; www.schaubuehne.de), which has a long anti-establishment tradition and has fostered the careers of many famous German actors over the years. Another important, though more venerable institution is the Deutsches Theater *(see p.70)*. Also worth mentioning is its spin-off venue, the Kammerspiele, which actually stages the more provocative productions.

The name Bertolt Brecht is closely associated with the city. His Berliner Ensemble *(see p.70)*, which the playwright founded and initially directed, continues to stage his plays at the Theater am Schiffbauerdamm. Perhaps the most artistically interesting productions of the 21st century, however, have been staged at the Volksbühne (Rosa-Luxemburg-Platz; www.volksbuehne-berlin. de), whose director Frank Castorff has had a long run of successes.

Variety and Comedy Theatres

What Berlin may lack in English-language theatre, it makes up in comedy and variety productions. Some are lavish, state-subsidised affairs; others are quirky independent shows, often with an offbeat message.

Perhaps the most established venue is the Friedrichstadtpalast *(see p.69 and 119)*, which offers a German take on the Las Vegas-meets-Paris extravaganza. Everything is executed with perfect German precision, but it can also seem a little soulless at times. Its main competitor is the Admiralspalast

Tickets
Tickets to classical concerts can be bought at the box office of the relevant concert hall, or through 'Theater-kassen' (ticket agencies). Note that many of the latter will charge a hefty commission on top of the price of the ticket. An alternative, however, is Hekticket – a good bet for last-minute tickets at discounted rates for same-day performances (Hardenbergstrasse 29d, Charlottenburg; tel: 030-230 9930; www.hekticket.de).

(see p.68 and 118), which presents a varied diet of musicals, concerts and other live acts. Then there is the more alternative Varieté Chamäleon (see p.65 and 120). Many find its shows much funnier than its more establishment big sisters.

One of Berlin's specialities, however, is small-scale cabaret. Among the most engaging of these is the Bar Jeder Vernunft (Schaperstrasse 24; see p.118), whose intimate venue is a 1920s tent. Many of the shows are a mixture of stand-up comedy and songs.

Musicals

Berlin's main venues for musicals are the historic Theater des Westens (see p.120) and the Musical Theater am Potsdamer Platz (see p.119). These both host long-running shows – usually German productions of international hits. Otherwise the Schillertheater often presents productions by touring companies.

MUSIC

Classical Music

When it comes to classical music, Berlin is one of the world's leading centres. With three opera houses, several world-class symphony orchestras and numerous acoustically excellent venues, the city offers audiences performances of a high standard almost every night.

Among the leading institutions is the State Opera (Staatsoper; see p.55 and 120), with its orchestra, the

Left: powerful stuff at Absinthe Depot.

Staatskapelle Berlin, under the direction of Daniel Barenboim. Then there is the Berlin Philharmonic, directed by Sir Simon Rattle and often hailed as the world's number one orchestra. Moreover, its home concert hall, the Philharmonie *(see p.47 and 119)* in Tiergarten, is renowned for its acoustics. Book well in advance, however, as concert tickets sell out extremely quickly.

In summer, the city offers open-air concerts of classical music, notably with the Philharmonic Orchestra at the Waldbühne, an amphitheatre seating 20,000 people near the Olympic Stadium. Equally impressive is the Classic Open Air concert series on historic Gendarmenmarkt *(see p.71)*.

Jazz

Berlin also has a highly diversified jazz scene, with live acts performing at venues such as A-Trane *(see p.121)*, Quasimodo *(see p.121)*, Flöz and b-flat. Celebrated local performers include the trumpet player Til Brönner and rising star saxophonist Mark Wyand.

Rock, Pop and World Music

Internationally renowned artists usually pay a visit to Berlin when touring Germany. Venues for the biggest live acts are the Olympic Stadium *(see p.121)*, the O2 World Arena *(see p.121)* and the Max-Schmeling-Halle.

In addition, the city has a strong tradition of independent rock, pop and blues. There is also a thriving World Music community of both homegrown and visiting artists. Kreuzberg and Neukölln, with their large immigrant populations, have produced a new generation of German rap and soul musicians as well.

Of course, Berlin would not be the same without its club music. Its thriving culture of dance, club, electro, house, techno and ambient music is the envy of Europe. Many big-name

Below: spinning the decks at a Berlin club.

artists live and perform in the city, and countless aficionados of the various styles flock to Berlin to check out all the latest developments.

FILM

Berlin has been Germany's cinema capital since the medium was invented. Classics include Fritz Lang's *Metropolis* (1927) and Josef von Sternberg's *The Blue Angel* (1930). The UFA Studios in nearby Babelsberg produced some of the most famous and, during the Nazi era, notorious films Germany has made.

The majority of Berlin's big cinemas play dubbed versions of Hollywood films. However, the Cinestar at the Sony Center *(see p.120)*, the Arsenal *(see p.120)* and the Cinemaxx, all located around Potsdamer Platz, frequently screen films in their original-language versions with German subtitles. The best way to find out what is on is to pick up a listings magazine such as *tip* or *Zitty* and look for films labelled *OF* (*Orignalfassung*, original version), *OmU* (*Original mit Untertiteln*, original with subtitles) or, for non-German or English-language films, *O m engl U*, indicating English subtitles. Note that cinemas tend to use the German titles for films even when they are going to be screening them in English.

If you are visiting in February, the Berlinale will be in full swing. This prestigious film festival is held annually and exhibits major new films from around the world. Directors and producers vie to win the Golden Bear award for best film. Members of the public are able to attend screenings, but it is wise to make your plans several months in advance. The event runs a comprehensive website (www.berlinale.de) with all the information you will need about what is on and how to get tickets.

NIGHTLIFE

To survive a night out in Berlin, get some sleep first. The city does not have any closing hours – you will hardly ever hear a 'last call' in a bar – and clubs do not get interesting until well after midnight. Moreover, you will not have to worry about getting around. Public transport will take you close to the action, and there are plenty of late buses to ferry you back home again. At weekends most U- and S-Bahn train lines also offer an all-night service.

Some of the city's best bars, pubs and clubs can be found in Mitte's Scheunenviertel and Spandauer Vorstadt. It is generally, though, the clubs of Friedrichshain that foster the latest cutting-edge trends. Meanwhile, a more alternative and laid-back crowd hangs out in Prenzlauer Berg and Kreuzberg. West Berlin – with the notable exception of Schöneberg, which has some good bars and plays host to the gay scene – is far more subdued, with some chic bars but few clubs.

Above from far left: a busy drinking hole; Berlin has a plethora of stylish bars.

Cabaret
Filmed on location in West Berlin and in other parts of Germany, Bob Fosse's 1972 adaptation of the musical *Cabaret* remains both popular and critically acclaimed to this day. The original musical was itself adapted from Christopher Isherwood's *Berlin Stories* and subsequent play, *I am a Camera*. However, it is the film version's portrayal of Berlin during the Weimar Republic that most influences how visitors imagine the city before they arrive and experience the reality.

HISTORY: KEY DATES

There can be few cities more evocative of modern European history than Berlin. Almost everywhere you look, you are reminded of the past, whether the glories of Frederick the Great or the annihilation of World War II.

EARLY HISTORY

1237	First record of Berlin and Cölln on two Spree river islands.
1432	The two settlemens are united and consolidated as one city.
1618–48	Thirty Years War and plague halve Berlin's population.
1640	The Great Elector, Friedrich Wilhelm, occupies the throne and sets out to turn Prussia into a European superpower.
1685	The Edict of Potsdam attracts 15,000 Huguenots from France to Berlin and Brandenburg.
1740	Frederick II (later 'the Great') becomes Prussian king and turns Potsdam into a Prussian Versailles.
1756–63	Prussia emerges victorious from the Seven Years War.
1786	Death of Frederick the Great.

19TH AND EARLY 20TH CENTURIES

1806	Napoleon defeats Prussia and occupies Berlin, taking the Quadriga (horses and chariot) from atop the Brandenburg Gate back to France.
1813	Napoleon is defeated at Grossbeeren and Leipzig.
1848	The Quadriga is returned to Berlin.
1848	March Revolution is brutally crushed.
1871	Bismarck makes Berlin the Imperial capital of the united Germany after victory in the Franco-Prussian War.
1914–18	Kaiser Wilhelm II starts World War I. Germany's eventual defeat brings revolution and the end of the monarchy.
1919	The Weimar Republic is established.

HITLER'S BERLIN

1933	Hitler becomes Chancellor of Germany.
1936	Berlin hosts the Olympic Games.

Cabbages
When Friedrich Wilhelm I came to the throne, a wag's graffiti on the palace wall pinpointed the costs of his parents' extravagance: 'This castle is for rent and the royal residence of Berlin for sale.' To pay off the debts, he cut court officials' salaries from 250,000 silver thalers to 50,000, sold the opulent coronation robes, melted down the palace silver, and tore the flowers out of Schloss Charlottenburg Park and replaced them with a far more practical crop: cabbages.

1938	Kristallnacht pogrom on 9 November.
1939–45	World War II is planned and directed from Berlin.
1943	Berlin experiences its first heavy Allied bombing raids.
1945	After fierce street-fighting with the Red Army, Germany finally surrenders unconditionally.

Above from far left: Frederick the Great's Schloss Sanssouci *(see p.90)*; the Berlin Wall at the East Side Gallery *(see p.89)*.

POST-WORLD WAR II: BERLIN DIVIDED

1945–7	Berlin is divided and governed by the four Allied Powers of Britain, France, the US and USSR.
1948–9	Berlin Airlift. The Soviets cut off transport access to West Berlin (the three Western Allied sectors). US and British aeroplanes keep the city supplied for 11 months.
1953	Uprising in East Berlin is suppressed by Soviet troops.
1961	The Wall is built on 13 August by the East German authorities.
1963	US President John F. Kennedy visits West Berlin and renews US commitment to the city with the words, 'Ich bin ein Berliner'.
1968	Left-wing and anti-war protests take place in West Berlin, making it a focal point for Germany's student and hippie movements.
1971	Erich Honecker becomes head of state in East Germany. An agreement between the four Allied Powers formalises the city's division, but allows for West Germans to visit the East more easily.
1987	US President Ronald Reagan visits West Berlin and demands that the Brandenburg Gate be opened.

THE FALL OF THE WALL AND BEYOND

1989	The GDR government collapses and the Wall comes down on 9 November.
1990	The two halves of Germany are reunited on 3 October.
1992	The German parliament makes Berlin the new seat of government, though the transfer of all the machinery of state takes until 2003.
2006	Berlin's new central railway station, the monumental Hauptbahnhof, is completed.
2008	The festive opening of the US Embassy at Pariser Platz marks the completion of the city's premier architectural landmark.
2009	The World Athletics Championships are held in the stadium originally built for the 1936 Olympic Games.

Famous Berliners
- August Borsig, industrialist, 1804–54.
- Marlene Dietrich, actress, 1901–92.
- Lion Feuchtwanger, writer, 1884–1958.
- Walter Gropius, architect, 1883–1969.
- Wolfgang Joop, designer, 1944–.
- Hildegard Knef, actress and singer, 1925–2002.
- Robert Koch, virologist, 1843–1910.
- Max Liebermann, painter, 1847–1935.
- Heinrich Mann, writer, 1871–1950.
- Helmut Newton, photographer, 1920–2004.
- Johann Gottfried Schadow, architect, 1764–1850.
- Anna Seghers, writer, 1900–83.
- Werner von Siemens, industrialist, 1816–1892.
- Kurt Tucholsky, writer, 1890–1935.
- Rachel Varnhagen, writer, 1771–1833.
- Heinrich Zille, painter, 1858–1929.

WALKS AND TOURS

BERLIN HIGHLIGHTS BY BUS

This tour combines the highlights of a number of the other walks in this book. It's a good one to do if you only have a few hours for sightseeing and want to see the sights quickly, or if you just want to get your bearings.

Bargain Sightseeing
Bus routes 100 or 200 are the cheapest way of taking in all major sights – the bus fare is just €2.10 for an adult, and the ticket is valid for two hours. Within that period, you can exit and re-enter the bus as often as you like, but only in one direction. Tickets are available at the BVG pavilion in front of Bahnhof Zoo S-Bahn station, or on the bus itself. To get to the upper deck, always take the front staircase, never the one at the back, which is only used for going down again.

DISTANCE 6km (3½ miles)
TIME 30 mins to a full day (see note below)
START Bahnhof Zoo
END Alexanderplatz
POINTS TO NOTE
All the areas and sights on this tour are covered in greater detail in walks 2 to 9 of this book. Food and Drink recommendations (shown in blue boxes) are included within those more detailed tours, but not repeated here. More detailed maps are also included in the other tours. The actual time spent on the bus is very short – either just half an hour on line 100 or 40 minutes on line 200. The length of the full tour – and the exact distance covered – will obviously depend on how much time you spend sightseeing off the bus.

You can take one of two buses – either the no. 100 or the no. 200 – on this tour, but the no. 100 is the more direct. (no. 200 detours slightly through the modern shopping and entertainment area around Potsdamer Platz and the museums in the Kulturforum.) The map shows the route taken by the no. 100 and the key sights described.

Both buses start in the square in front of **Bahnhof Zoo ❶**, the city's busiest bus station and the gateway to the Western downtown area. Bahnhof Zoo used to be West Berlin's central railway station, but now only serves the S-Bahn.

BREITSCHEIDPLATZ

Bus 100 leaves the area by turning right and then heading south to its first stop at **Breitscheidplatz ❷**, the bustling centre of downtown Western Berlin. Hop off the bus if you want to explore the square and the road west of it.

Kaiser-Wilhelm Memorial Church
Overshadowing the square is the ruined tower of the neo-Gothic **Kaiser-Wilhelm Gedächtniskirche ❸** *(see p.33)*, built in 1891–5 in memory of Kaiser Wilhelm I. Only its bell tower remains – a sober reminder of World War II – following heavy bombing attacks.

THE KU'DAMM

On the square's western side is the **Kurfürstendamm** ('Ku'damm' for short), the city's major shopping boulevard, laid out in the late 19th century in the style of the Champs-Elysées in Paris. In the 1920s, the thoroughfare and the surrounding streets evolved into a glamorous entertainment neighbourhood, but the damage was considerable during World War II, and the area lost its shine.

Since the fall of the Wall, the Ku'damm has weathered tough times, being less attractive than areas that were opening up in the former East Berlin. However, things have been improving in recent years, with urban regeneration taking place and smart boutiques moving in. Regeneration has also taken place in the roads north and south of the Ku'damm, home to some fine 19th-century mansions.

If you need refreshment along here, a lovely place is the **Wintergarten-Café im Literaturhaus**, see ⑪①, p.35, although this is quite a walk if you don't want to head far from Breitscheidplatz.

TIERGARTEN

Back at Breitscheidplatz, hop back on the bus, which takes you to the diplomatic quarter *(see p.40)* near the city's main park, the **Tiergarten ❹**, in just a few minutes. Laid out in the 17th century by the Hohenzollern rulers, the Tiergarten served kings and emperors as a game reserve, before being transformed into a public park in the 19th century by Peter Joseph Lenné. It is now one the city's green lung, with highlights including a zoo and an aquarium (explored in full on tour 3, *see p.38*).

Get off the bus at the 'Nordische Botschaften' (Norwegian Embassy) stop and follow Hofjägerallee (to the left) into the park.

Victory Column

Hofjägerallee leads to the **Siegessäule ❺**, a 69m (227ft) high column, erected in 1873 to commemorate the German Empire and Prussia's victories over Austria, France and Denmark. There's an observation platform at the top, which offers fine views. Above this is the enormous golden angel of victory, nicknamed 'Goldelse' (Golden Else).

The Reichstag

From the Siegessäule, get back on the bus again. You'll drive past **Schloss Bellevue** *(see p.41)*, then, on John-Foster-Dulles Allee, past the elegant 1950s **Haus der Kulturen der Welt** *(see p.42)*, a cultural centre identifiable by its sweeping roof. The next big sight en route, however, is the **Reichstag ❻** (parliament; *see p.42*). Get off the bus again if you want to explore it further.

Inside, the acclaimed glass cupola – added by British architect Lord Foster in 1997–9 – offers breathtaking views over Berlin's skyline as well as a good

Above from far left: the Victory Column; inside the Reichstag's dome; the Tiergarten.

Above: crowds on Kurfürstendamm; Kaiser-Wilhelm Gedächtniskirche; pelican at the zoo (in the Tiergarten).

look down inside the parliament chamber. If you're hungry at this point, you can eat at the restaurant in the Reichstag, **Käfer im Reichstag**, see ⑪④, p.42.

BRANDENBURG GATE

A few steps south from the Reichstag is the iconic city symbol, the neoclassical **Brandenburger Tor** ❼ (Brandenburg Gate; *see p.50*), built between 1788 and 1791 by Carl Gotthard Langhans as a triumphal arch and city gate on the road to Brandenburg.

Walk through the gate from west to east and stop on the square behind it, the **Pariser Platz** ❽ *(see p.51)*, the site of several embassies, a gallery and the deluxe Hotel Adlon *(see p.52)*. There are a couple of good cafés on the square: **Café Theodor Tucher** and **Café Akademie der Künste Pariser Platz**, see ⑪① and ⑪②, p.51.

UNTER DEN LINDEN

Running east from the Pariser Platz is **Unter den Linden**, a broad boulevard lined with historic monuments, state buildings and the lime trees after which it is named. First laid out as a riding path between the Tiergarten and the City Palace in the 16th century, it evolved as the Prussian, then the Imperial, capital's central thor-

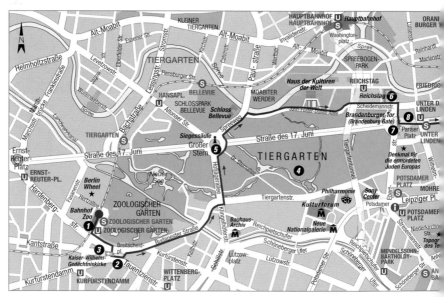

oughfare in the mid-17th century, making it the social, cultural and political centre of Berlin.

The bus stops frequently along here, making it easy for you to get on and off for sightseeing as you please. The key sights on Unter den Linden are explored in full on tour 6 *(see p.54)*, but if you just want to see the highlights, get off the no. 100 at the 'Staatsoper' stop.

This takes you to the **Staatsoper** ❾ (State Opera House; *see p.55*) and the historic buildings of the Forum Fridericianum, the architectural and cultural heart of historic centre of the former Prussian capital. For a coffee stop in this area, try the **Operncafé im Opernpalais**, see ⑪②, p.57.

500 m / 550 yds

MUSEUM ISLAND TO ALEXANDERPLATZ

Located slightly to the east of here, along Unter den Linden, is the Unesco-protected **Museumsinsel** ❿ (Museum Island), home to a concentration of national museums, the **Bode-Museum**, **Pergamonmuseum**, **Neues Museum**, **Alte Nationalgalerie** and **Altes Museum**, covered in full on tour 7 *(see p.60)*.

Schlossplatz and Nikolaiviertel

Pick up the bus again to cross the island. You'll head over the Schlossbrücke, to the right of which is the **Schlossplatz** ⓫ (Castle Square), once the site of several royal palaces, hence the name.

Before the bus stops at its final destination, you will pass Berlin City Hall, the **Rathaus** ⓬ *(see p.59)* and the quaint, historic **Nikolaiviertel** (Nicholas Quarter; *see p.58*), which should give you a good impression of what late 17th-century Berlin looked like (although note that many of the buildings here are reconstructions).

Alexanderplatz

From here, you can either walk or take the bus further east to its final stop, **Alexanderplatz** ⓭. Once you reach the square, there's another opportunity to take a look at the Berlin skyline, with a ride up the **Fernsehturm** (Television Tower), topped by a revolving café, see ⑪⑤, p.59.

Above from far left: exterior of the Alte Nationalgalerie; cycling by the Brandenburg Gate; the television tower on Alexanderplatz; detail of the Alte Nationalgalerie.

Above: Pergamonmuseum and the River Spree; the historic Nikolaikirche.

CHARLOTTENBURG

This tour heads to the district of Charlottenburg, formerly the heart of West Berlin. Highlights here include the city's major shopping avenue, the Kurfürstendamm, the largest department store in Europe (KaDeWe), fine 19th-century mansions and a legendary 'Currywurst' kiosk.

Commemorative Plaques

When strolling the streets of Charlottenburg-Wilmersdorf, you will often notice small white plaques with blue text, commemorating famous writers, scientists, actors and politicians who once lived and worked here. Among the most famous are the physician Robert Koch, the engineer Gottfried Daimler, the writers Joseph Roth, Kurt Tucholsky and Robert Musil and silent movie star Asta Nielsen.

DISTANCE 3km (2 miles)

TIME A full day

START Breitscheidplatz

END Savignyplatz

POINTS TO NOTE

To reach the starting point of the tour, take the U- or S-Bahn to the Zoologischer Garten. The Kurfürstendamm itself gets very crowded on Friday afternoons and Saturday mornings, making this walk more relaxed if you can do it on a weekday.

The large district of Charlottenburg makes up much of the Western downtown area, running east–west from the Tiergarten to Spandau and north–west from Tegel airport to the district of Wilmersdorf. It is cut by the city's major shopping boulevard, the Kurfürstendamm ('Ku'damm' for short). This 2.2km (1½ mile) long avenue was laid out in the late 19th century and modelled on the Champs-Elysées in Paris, as the planners of the new capital of the German Empire wanted to compete with the splendour of other European cities.

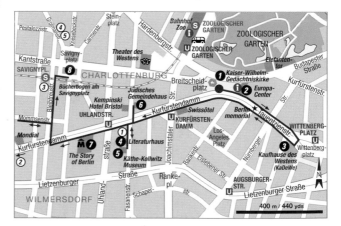

Even by Berlin standards, this area of the city is fairly young – some hundred years ago it was called the 'New West'. The wealthy upper classes preferred at that time to settle in the historic eastern quarter of Berlin, and it was only in the 1920s that the Ku'-damm evolved into a glitzy shopping and entertainment strip.

Later that century, World War II ravaged the fine Jugendstil mansions here, although many have now been restored, if not on the Ku'damm itself then on the more elegant side streets to the north and south. Since the fall of the Wall, Charlottenburg and the Ku'damm have weathered tough times, as the Mitte area further east attracted visitors and locals instead. In recent years, however, the buzz has been coming back to the West, with urban regeneration under way and elegant boutiques moving in.

BREITSCHEIDPLATZ

The centre of downtown Western Berlin is **Breitscheidplatz**, a busy square that can easily be reached via the Zoologischer Garten station (U- and S-Bahn). From the station, head across Budapester Strasse, the wide street in front, in the direction of the high-rise buildings surrounding the square. Street artists, performers and vendors, teenagers with their skateboards, political demonstrators and all sorts of people trying to be heard make this square the vibrant heart of West Berlin.

In summer, the 1980s Weltkugel-brunnen (Globe Fountain), a granite water fountain on the square dubbed 'water burger' for its chunky, rounded shape, offers cool respite.

Kaiser-Wilhelm Memorial Church
Overshadowing the square is the ruined tower of the **Kaiser-Wilhelm Gedächtniskirche ❶** (tel: 030-218 5023; www.gedaechtniskirche-berlin. de; daily 9am–7pm; free), built in 1891–5 in memory of Kaiser Wilhelm I. The neo-Gothic church was bombed in an air raid in 1943, however, and all that remains is its bell tower; its ruins have been left standing, after Berliners voted for this as a reminder of war. Inside the bell tower is an exhibition on the horrors of the war.

Next to the tower is a 1960s church. Pop inside to admire the glorious blue light inside – this is particularly fine on late summer afternoons.

Europa-Center
Facing the church to the east is the **Europa-Center ❷** (tel: 030-2649 7940; www.europa-center-berlin.de; Mon–Thur 10am–8pm, Fri 10am–9pm, Sat 10am–8pm), a high-rise crowned with the revolving star of the Mercedes car manufacturer. Although the building now looks outdated, it remains a symbol of a Western city resurrected in the 1960s in the face of Socialist East Germany. Inside are boutiques, food and multimedia stores as

Above from far left: historic buildings on the Ku'damm; Kaiser-Wilhelm Gedächtniskirche.

well as pleasant cafés. Note the *Clock of Flowing Time*, an artwork by the French artist Bernard Gitton in which neon-coloured liquids show the time. Enter the building from the square and exit at its Tauentzienstrasse doors, where a chunk of the Berlin Wall is on show.

TAUENTZIENSTRASSE

Once you have exited the Europa-Center, you will be standing on **Tauentzienstrasse**, a short stretch dominated by inexpensive fashion shops. Turn left onto the boulevard and walk east towards the huge metal monument in the middle of the street. The 1987 tubular steel *Berlin* memorial comprises two split links of a chain, symbolising the city's division.

At the end of Tauentzienstrasse is Wittenbergplatz. Once a historic spot,

it is now a rather unpleasant square with 1970s high-rise blocks. The only relief is the beautifully restored neoclassical Wittenbergplatz (U-Bahn) station, dating from 1910–13. The interior, complete with old-style billboards and ticket counters, is like a time capsule.

Kaufhaus des Westens

After a visit to Wittenbergplatz turn back onto Tauentzienstrasse and walk towards the monumental **Kaufhaus des Westens ❸** (KaDeWe; Tauentzien-strasse; tel: 030-21210; www.kadewe. de; Mon–Thur 10am–8pm, Fri 10am–9pm, Sat 9.30am–8pm), founded in 1907. Dubbed 'KaDeWe' – rather less of a mouthful than the full name – the store is seven storeys high and 60,000 sq m (646 sq ft), making it the largest department store in Europe.

Heavily damaged in World War II, the department store was reopened in 1950 and has undergone several facelifts since then – the last one in 2007. Those looking for the latest international fashion or accessories should not be disappointed, but pride of place goes to the food department – the largest of its kind in the world– on the sixth floor. The selection of fresh produce from across the world – including 1,300 cheeses and 1,200 types of sausages – is spectacular. Take time to enjoy the demonstration areas, where you can sample oysters, sushi, bouillabaisse, lobster and other such tasty delicacies.

Below: *Berlin*, representing the city divided, on Tauentzienstrasse.

ON AND AROUND THE KURFÜRSTENDAMM

After a visit to KaDeWe, it is time for more sightseeing. Leave the department store by the Tauentzienstrasse exit and turn left, walking back towards Breitscheidplatz. Passing the square, you will finally hit the **Ku'damm**.

Passing vast multimedia stores such as Hugendubel and department stores including Wertheim on your right, cross **Joachimstaler Strasse** on your left. This is one of the busiest street corners in West Berlin. Just behind you is the **Ku'damm Eck** (meaning 'Ku'damm Corner'), home to the Swissôtel and a budget fashion department store; adjacent is the sleek Hotel Concorde. The triangular glass-and-steel building is the **Neues Kranzler-Eck** by German–American architect Helmut Jahn.

Fasanenstrasse

Continue for a while on the Ku'damm until you hit Fasanenstrasse. Turn left into this leafy side street, lined with grand late 19th-century mansions. Among the villas still intact here is the **Literaturhaus** ❹ (23 Fasanenstrasse; tel: 030-882 5414; www. literaturhaus-berlin.de; daily 9.30am–1am; free), a literary centre set back slightly from the road. If you're feeling peckish at this point, stop at the **Wintergarten-Café im Literaturhaus**, see ⑪①.

Arty types may like to pop next door to the **Käthe-Kollwitz-Museum** ❺

(Fasanenstrasse 24; tel: 030-882 5210; www.kaethe-kollwitz.de; Mon, Wed–Sun 11am–6pm; charge), dedicated to the work of the artist (1867–1945). *(For more on Käthe Kollwitz, see p.86.)*

Now turn around and head back north up Fasanenstrasse, crossing over the Ku'damm (Fasanenstrasse continues on the other side of the main boulevard). On the corner of the two streets, you'll pass the Kempinski Hotel Bristol, a popular meeting point for jet-setters in the 1950s and 1960s, although now something of a corporate-looking place.

Opposite it is the **Jüdisches Gemeindehaus** ❻ (tel: 030-880 280; www.jg-berlin.org; daily 8am–6pm, Fri 8am–3pm; free), a centre for the Jewish community. Note the red sandstone entrance – the arch is all that survives from the original 1912 synagogue. Built in a Roman Byzantine style by Ehrenfried Hessel, it was once Germany's largest Jewish temple, but was brutally looted on 9 November 1938, on Kristallnacht – a Nazi-orches-

Above from far left: Mary-Janes at KaDeWe; taking a break at the Café im Literaturhaus.

Did You Know?

The Ku'damm starts with house no. 11. Sections of the road were moved to help traffic flow in the 1920s, and the first 10 house numbers were simply dropped.

Food and Drink 🍴

① WINTERGARTEN-CAFÉ IM LITERATURHAUS

Fasanenstr. 23; tel: 030-882 5414; www.literaturhaus-berlin.de; daily 9.30am–1am; €€

One of the most charming cafés in Western Berlin, this historic café in the city's literary centre welcomes a mix of writers, media types and visitors alike. The winter garden setting, where delicious traditional German 'Kaffee und Kuchen' as well as light lunch or dinner are served, is completed by a lovely garden.

Kantstrasse Architecture

On Kantstrasse, near Savignyplatz, two high-rise buildings catch the eye. The grand neoclassical Theater des Westens was built by Bernhard Sehring in 1895–6. It now hosts changing musical productions. The other building, just opposite, is the contemporary Kant-Dreieck, identifiable by the huge aluminium sail on the roof.

trated attack on Jewish institutions and shops. The remains of the synagogue were later hit by Allied bombs in 1943.

Story of Berlin

Now walk back onto the Ku'damm, turning right (west) out of Fasanenstrasse. Walk westwards and keep going until you see the wing of an aeroplane sticking up vertically out of the pavement. This marks the entrance to **The Story of Berlin** ❼ (tel: 030–8872 0100; www.story-of-berlin. de; daily 10am–8pm; charge), a multimedia exhibition on the history of Berlin. Some of the displays are located underground in a huge nuclear shelter built to house around 3,500 people by the anti-Soviets in the 1970s.

NORTH TOWARDS SAVIGNYPLATZ

Emerge from the darkness of the nuclear bunker and head further west along the Ku'damm. At this point on the avenue the shops and boutiques become more upmarket, with fewer chains and a concentration of chic fashion, shoes and jewellery stores.

Not all the attractions here have the sheen of exclusivity, though. After you pass Bleibtreustrasse, look out for the neon signs of **Ku'damm 195**, see ⑪②, an 'Imbiss' (snack kiosk), serving 'Currywurst', curried sausage – something of a Berlin speciality *(see p.14)*. This place is something of a local

legend, and is decorated with photographs of celebrity visitors – German and international – who have enjoyed a sausage or two here.

Bleibtreustrasse

For the moment, get back onto the Ku'damm, then turn right into **Bleibtreustrasse**, one of the most attractive side streets in this part of town. Many of its buildings remained unscathed during World War II or have been meticulously restored, giving you a good impression of how this part of Berlin would have looked prior to the devastation of the war.

Walk north along Bleibtreustrasse until you hit Mommsenstrasse – another pretty side street. You may want to venture along Mommenstrasse at this point – or just continue along Bleibtreustrasse until you get to the S-Bahn bridge. You'll pass the tiny **Lubitsch**, see ⑪③, a great place for a quick lunch, if you resisted the Currywurst at Ku'damm 195.

Just in front of Lubitsch, a small alley leads parallel to the tracks of the S-Bahn, past cosy cafés, bookstores and antiques shops. Walk along here to reach Savignyplatz.

Savignyplatz

On first arrival, **Savignyplatz** ❽ feels less like a square than the meeting point of three streets. The two-lane Kantstrasse (on your left) cuts the square into two halves. On the

northern side are inviting park benches. You might also venture into the three streets that run off from here: Grolmannstrasse, Knesebeckstrasse and Carmerstrasse. On these three streets (and on Savignyplatz itself) are a range of chic shops, cafés, bars and restaurants, including **Café Savigny**, see ⑪④, that are popular with the neighbourhood's intellectual and arty crowd. This area is particularly good for people-watching.

Note that you might want to return here later in the evening for the lively atmosphere in eating/drinking holes such as **Florian**, see ⑪⑤.

For now, key an eye open for one of Berlin's best bookstores: Bücherbogen am Savignyplatz. Occupying three arches under the S-Bahn viaduct on the square, this well-established shop specialises in glossy coffee-table books, notably on art and photography, as well as rare magazines.

Above from far left: the Bristol Hotel Kempinski; art books at the Story of Berlin; on leafy Bleibtreustrasse.

Food and Drink

② KU'DAMM 195 CURRYWURST
Kurfürstendamm 195; tel: 030-881 8942; Mon–Sat 11am–5am, Sun noon–5am; €
This tiny Imbiss (snack kiosk) has been a landmark for more than 25 years. Spicy, filling Currywurst, a German speciality consisting of sliced boiled pork sausage covered under thick layers of tomato sauce, curry and pepper, served with French fries, either 'rot' (red) or 'weisse' (white), ie with ketchup or mayonnaise, welcomes the Charlottenburg jet set. The 195 is the only place in the city where you can order this street-side delicacy with a Pommery champagne.

③ LUBITSCH
Bleibtreustrasse 47; tel: 030-882 3756; Mon–Sat 10am–1am, Sun 6pm–1am; €
An old-fashioned bohemian café with a restaurant, the tiny Lubitsch (named after a 1920s German film director, Ernst Lubitsch) is a favourite among local artists and intellectuals. They come here to enjoy the faded grandeur and such hearty, traditional Berlin dishes as liver with apples, tasty international cuisine and good cakes. In summer, the outside tables are great for people-watching.

④ CAFÉ SAVIGNY
Grolmanstrasse 53–4; tel: 030-3151 9612; 9am–1am; €
The upmarket Café Savigny has been a fixture on the neighbourhood scene for years now and is a popular rendez-vous point for the gay community. It offers great cakes and pastries and a fine selection of breakfast dishes. In summer, try to get a table outside for some good people-watching.

⑤ RESTAURANT FLORIAN
Grolmanstrasse 52; tel: 030-313 9184; www.restaurant-florian.de; daily 6pm–3am; €€
The Florian is a favourite late-night hangout for hungry actors and the local media crowd. Owner Gerti serves fresh, hearty sausages and poultry and game dishes from her Bavarian home region of Franken. The Nuremberg roasted sausages are strongly recommended.

TIERGARTEN

Tiergarten refers both to the district of that name and to the park. Its literal meaning – 'animal garden' - hints at the origins of this expansive green space covering 250ha (630 acres) between downtown East and West Berlin.

DISTANCE 3.75km (3⅕ miles)
TIME A full day
START Zoologischer Garten
END Reichstag
POINTS TO NOTE
To get to the starting point, catch a U- or S-Bahn to Bahnhof Zoo. Alternatively, the heart of the Tiergarten area can also be reached by train to the Tiergarten S-Bahn station, off Strasse des 17 Juni, just a few steps away from the park.

Above: relaxing at Schleusenkrug; the elaborately carved Elefantor entrance to the zoo.

Laid out in the 17th century by the Hohenzollern rulers, the Tiergarten served kings and emperors as a game reserve before being transformed into a public park in the 19th century by Peter Joseph Lenné. Nowadays, it's the city's most popular green space, and in summer its shady groves and meadows invite people from all walks of life. Barbecues are popular here, and even the Federal President, who once complained about the smell, has not been able to change this longstanding tradition. Some areas of the park are popular for nude sunbathing. In the evening, the park turns into Berlin's main cruising area for members of the gay community. This tour covers its highlights.

BERLIN ZOO

The tour starts at the Zoologischer Garten U- and S-Bahn station, which owes its name to **Zoo Berlin ❶** (Berlin Zoo; Hardenbergplatz 8; tel: 030-254 010; www.zoo-berlin.de; Jan–mid-Mar 9am–5pm, mid-Mar–mid-Sept 9am–7.30pm, mid-Sept–late Oct 9am–7pm, late Oct–Dec 9am–5pm; charge), whose western entrance is just a few steps away from the station, across the car park.

Note that if you need a bite to eat in this area, **Schleusenkrug**, see ⑪①, is just behind the zoo.

Zoo Highlights

Founded in 1844, the zoo is one of the oldest and largest animal parks in the world. More than 1,400 species, and some 15,000 animals, are housed in its enclosures, some of which are historic, others of which are 'state-of-the-art'. Highlights include the ape house, the giraffe house, the elephant houses and the polar bear enclosure – made famous in 2006 when the cute baby polar bear Knut was born here (the first polar bear born in the zoo in more than 30 years). As is the case in many zoos, some of the enclosures are rather depressing, particularly on grey days, with animals which look disturbed and frustrated in their restricted surroundings. A visit here may not appeal to everyone.

Exit the zoo through the eastern gate, the intricately carved stone 'Elefantentor' (Elephant Gate).

Aquarium

From here, turn left and walk a few metres/yards to the **Aquarium** ❷ (Hardenbergplatz 8; tel: 030–254 010; www.aquarium-berlin.de; daily 9am–6pm; charge), which forms part of the zoo. It presents myriad kinds of fish, from tropical ones to freshwater types, as well as insects, snakes, reptiles and creepy-crawlies of various kinds. A highlight is the alligator hall, a rather musty, humid greenhouse, where vis-

Above from far left: polar bear paws at the zoo; lazing in the Reichstag; Victory Column; cycling in the Tiergarten.

Big Wheel

Close to the zoo, on Hertzallee, is Europe's largest ferris wheel, the Great Berlin Wheel (www.greatwheel. com; charge), set to open at some point in the future. At 185m (607ft) high, it will be some 50m (164 ft) taller than the London Eye. Visitors will take 35-minute rotations in one of the wheel's 36 gondolas (each with room for 40) for great views of the city.

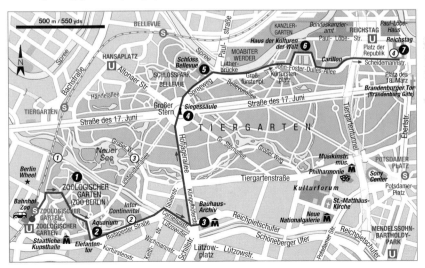

itors can walk along a wooden platform above an artificial river in which alligators laze.

EMBASSY QUARTER

From the aquarium, head along Budapester Strasse, a busy and rather unattractive road leading into the heart of the Tiergarten. On your left, you will pass the **Intercontinental Hotel** *(see p.111)*, one of Western Berlin's leading luxury hotels. There are great views of the Tiergarten from the hotel, and it also houses one of the city's top restaurants, **Hugo's**, see ②.

As the road curves round slightly,

Below: glittering 'Goldelse' atop the Victory Column.

you may spot the first of several embassies, including those of Norway, Japan and Italy, in this area. The attractive setting and the proximity of this area to, first, the palaces of the Imperial rulers and, since the 1990s, the Federal German government to the east of the park, attracted many such institutions to this area.

BAUHAUS ARCHIVE

Turn right onto Corneliusstrasse, then cross Klingelhöferstrasse, home to the Modernist **Bauhaus-Archiv** ❸ (Klingelhöferstrasse 14; tel: 030-254 0020; www.bauhaus.de; Wed–Mon 10am–5pm; charge). Designed by Walter Gropius, the flat-walled concrete building is devoted to the design, art and architecture of the Bauhaus school that revolutionised design in the 1920s, producing numerous modern classics.

NEUER SEE

Back on Klingelhöfer, walk north until the road becomes Hofjägerallee. Continue heading north until you hit the Grosser Weg to your left. As one of the most attractive little paths crisscrossing the park, it will lead you deep into the woods to the Neuer See (New Lake) and the **Café am Neuen See**, see ⑪③ – an ideal spot for a late breakfast or a lunch break.

From here, you can either walk back the way you came or take one of the

many paths leading north to Strasse des 17 Juni (its name commemorates the uprising of workers in Socialist East Germany against Soviet domination on 17 June 1953). En route, you may notice houseboats moored on the water here.

VICTORY COLUMN

Either way will lead you to the centre of the Tiergarten and the **Siegessäule** ❹ (Grosser Stern 1; tel: 030-391 2961; www.monument-tales.de; Apr–Oct: Mon–Fri 9.30am–6.30pm, Sat, Sun 9.30am–7pm, Nov–Mar: Mon–Fri 10am–5pm, Sat, Sun 10am–5.30pm; charge), a a 69m (227ft) high victory column. This unabashed monument to Prussian militarism was completed in 1873, two years after the victory over the French, and also marks successes against Denmark (1864) and Austria (1866).

It originally stood in front of the Reichstag but was moved here (and increased in height) by Hitler, who wanted to turn the Strasse des 17 Juni into a grand east–west axis once the war had been won. From all the grandeur of Nazi fantasy only the street lamps, designed by Hitler's favourite architect Albert Speer, have survived.

The view from the top observation platform can be reached via 285 winding steps. If you've got a head for heights, it's worth the effort for the excellent 360-degree views of the Tiergarten. Just above you from this point is the huge golden angel with spread wings and a spear and laurel wreath in its hands and is nicknamed 'Goldelse' (Golden Elsie).

SCHLOSS BELLEVUE

Back on *terra firma*, take the under-path from the Siegessäule to the north onto Spreeweg, where you will pass the neoclassical **Schloss Bellevue** ❺ (www. bundespraesident.de). Built in 1785 for a brother of the Prussian King Frederick II, it has served as the Berlin seat of the German Federal President since the late 1950s. It became the President's main residence and office in 1994. The palace grounds are closed to the public, but the façade can be admired from the street.

Above from far left: fun for the kids at the zoo; taking time out in the Tiergarten; exterior and exhibits at the Bauhaus Archiv.

Food and Drink

② HUGO'S AT INTERCONTI
Hotel Interconti, Budapester Strasse 2; tel: 030-2602 1263; www.hugos-restaurant.de; Mon–Sat 6pm–10.30pm; €€€€
Located just outside the park, close to the aquarium entrance, this is one of Berlin's most stylish, yet intimate Michelin-starred restaurants. It is the only one in its class to offer great views of the Berlin skyline. The swift and friendly service (no stiff upper lip here, despite the prices), an excellent changing menu (French and international dishes) and possibly the best gourmet cheese selection in town make this a favourite with businessmen and tourists alike.

③ CAFÉ AM NEUEN SEE
Lichtensteinallee 2; tel: 030-2544 9330; daily from 10am; €€
The Café am Neuen See started out as an upscale breakfast café off the Neuer See in the heart of the Tiergarten, but has evolved into one of the city's largest and most popular beer gardens – great for a strong, cold beer and a barbecue. The atmosphere is often pretty lively, the clientele is more hip than traditional, and the location is unbeatable.

Wrapped Reichstag
In 1995 the Bulgarian-born, American-based artists Christo and his Moroccan-born wife and creative partner Jeanne-Claude gave the Reichstag their trademark wrapping treatment. They covered the German parliament with fire-resistant poly-propylene fabric and aluminium (tied with 15km/9 miles of rope) and turned it into a monumental work of art. The project was a great success for the city – despite fierce initial debate among German politicians on its pros and cons – and was ultimately admired by millions of visitors.

HAUS DER KULTUREN DER WELT

Opposite the palace, the pretty John-Foster-Dulles-Allee (right by the River Spree) leads back into the Tiergarten; after a few hundred metres/ yards, you will pass the elegant **Haus der Kulturen der Welt ❻** (House of World Cultures; John-Foster-Dulles-Allee 10; tel: 030–3978 7175; www.hkw.de; Mon–Sun 10am–9pm; price depends on events). West Berlin's former congress hall is a fine example of 1950s architecture and is notable for its striking curved-concrete roof, which has led Berliners to dub the building the 'pregnant oyster'. The lauded roof did, however, collapse in 1979, but has since been restored. Today, the building serves as a multicultural exhibition centre and venue for events.

THE REICHSTAG

Further down the boulevard, after another bend, the **Reichstag ❼** (Platz der Republik; tel: 030-2273 2152; www.bundestag.de; daily 8am–midnight, last entry 10pm; free) will come into view. Built between 1884 and 1894 by Paul Wallot to house the new parliament of the united German Empire, the Reichstag later became the focal point for the political turmoil of the dying Weimar Republic. In 1933, the building fell victim to a fire (thought to have been sparked by a Communist), an event that was then used by the Nazis as a pretext for initiating large-scale political cleansing of their opponents.

The building was not used again until 1945 (the Nazi Reichstag, a mockery of a parliament, convened instead in the Kroll Opera, which once stood just adjacent), when Soviet troops stormed the empty hull and raised the red flag on the top.

In the years following World War II, the Reichstag was restored. When the Wall went up, however, it ran right behind the Reichstag, setting the building on the fringes of West Berlin; thereafter, it was used only occasionally – for political gatherings.

In 1990 came German unity, followed shortly by the decision to move the capital from Bonn to Berlin and to make the Reichstag the seat of parliament once again. After extensive restoration and the addition of a new dome (a nod to the one destroyed in the 1933 fire) by the British architect Norman (Lord) Foster in 1997–9, the Reichstag is now a winning marriage of old and new.

Food and Drink
④ KÄFER IM REICHSTAG
Platz der Republik; tel: 030-226 2990; www.feinkost-kaefer. de; daily 9–10.15am, noon–2.30pm, 3.30pm–4.30pm, 6.30pm–midnight; €€€
This restaurant on top of the Reichstag is the only public one in the German parliament and offers sweeping views of the Eastern downtown area and its historic landmarks. The pricey but tasty food is a mix of international and local dishes. Reservations are advised in the evenings and at weekends.

Visiting the Building

It's worth taking a tour of the building, even if you're not a huge fan of politics. The inside of the cupola offers breathtaking views over Berlin's skyline as well as a good look down inside the parliament chamber. You'll also get the chance to see original graffiti left here by Soviets and visiting GIs in 1945. If you need refreshment, the **Käfer im Reichstag**, see ⑪④, on the rooftop, is an impressive place for a break.

PAUL-LÖBE-HAUS AND CHANCELLERY

Back in front of the Reichstag, note the huge, modern building to the left of it. This is the Paul-Löbe-Haus, the main office complex for over 600 German members of parliament and their staff.

Chancellery

Opposite stands the architecturally striking Kanzleramt (Chancellery), the residence and office of the German Chancellor. Designed by Berlin architect Axel Schulte and completed in 2000, the huge grey, cube-like building has been the subject of considerable debate about the beauty of state buildings. As is typical of Berliners *(see p.47)*, they quickly found a nickname for it: Waschmaschine (washing machine), thanks to its oversized, round windows.

Behind the Kanzleramt is the Kanzlergarten, a lovely garden right next to the River Spree.

Above from far left: Reichstag dome; the building viewed from the front.

Glass Dome
The Reichstag's glass dome is designed to direct natural light and ventilation into the Bundestag chamber below; at night it reflects the artificial light coming from the chamber.

Hamburger Bahnhof

Just north of the Tiergarten park is the city's main contemporary art museum, the Hamburger Bahnhof-Museum für Gegenwart Berlin (Invalidenstrasse 50–1; tel: 030-397 8340; www.hamburgerbahnhof.de; Tue–Fri 10am–6pm, Sat 11am–8pm, Sun 11am–6pm; charge). It's slightly off the beaten track and rather out on a limb, by several very busy roads, but is definitely worth a visit from anyone interested in contemporary art. The museum is located within the former Hamburger Bahnhof mainline railway station, built in 1874 but by 1906 deemed too small and soon converted into a museum. After World War II it stood in a no man's land between East and West, and it was not until the late 1980s that plans were introduced to renovate it; the new museum finally opened in 1996. Covering art from the mid-20th century to the present, the collection, spread over two floors, includes works by Andy Warhol, Cy Twombly, Robert Rauschenberg, Roy Lichtenstein, Joseph Beuys, Anselm Kiefer and Dan Flavin. The eastern wing of the museum contains a lovely restaurant, with red banquettes, areas to browse magazines and a good light menu.

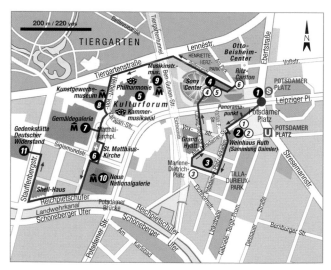

POTSDAMER PLATZ AND THE KULTURFORUM

The area around Potsdamer Platz, one of the city's main squares (in the Tier-garten district), is a reflection of a city resurrected. Highlights include the Sony Center, the Kulturforum arts complex and a memorial to German resistance.

DISTANCE 2km (1¼ miles)
TIME Half a day
START Potsdamer Platz
END Gedenkstätte Deutscher Widerstand
POINTS TO NOTE
If you are travelling to the starting point by public transport, take the U- or S-Bahn to Potsdamer Platz.

Right in the heart of Berlin, **Potsdamer Platz ❶** was historically one of the city's most impressive squares, and the hub of the city's nightlife in the 1920s and 1930s. It was bombed to rubble, however, in World War II, then lost in the no-man's land between East and West when the city was divided. Between 1961 and 1989, Potsdamer Platz was nothing but a wide, open space in the shadow of the Wall.

Did You Know?
The peculiar vertical glass tubes on Potsdamer Platz are the light and ventilation funnels for the S- and U-Bahn station under the pavement. Even more notable is an old-fashioned-looking, dark-green clock-cum-tower of traffic lights, a replica of a 1920s traffic light that once stood here and was the first automatic one of its kind.

All that changed rapidly, when history threw the square back into the centre of a reuniting capital. In the 1990s, the area evolved into a massive building site, when international corporations such as Sony, Daimler and ABB decided to develop it.

POTSDAMER PLATZ

Approaching Potsdamer Platz from the east or the north will offer the best views of its skyscrapers. In the middle is Potsdamer Platz 1, a red-brick highrise designed by Werner Kolhoff; for bird's eye views of the square, take the lift up to the observation platform in the tower (Panoramapunkt, Potsdamer Platz 1; tel: 030-2529 4372; www. panoramapunkt.de; daily 11am– 8pm; charge). To the right, adorned with the DB logo, is an office block housing the headquarters of the German railways (Deutsche Bundesbahn).

As you cross the square, look out for the narrow, cobblestoned line running across the street – this marks the former location of the Wall.

Alte Potsdamer Strasse

Now head south, onto Alte Potsdamer Strasse. At no. 5 is Weinhaus Huth, which managed to survive World War II. It now houses a wine bistro, **Lutter & Wegner**, see ⑪①, the **Diekmann** restaurant, see ⑪②, and the Daimler corporation's modern art collection, the **Sammlung Daimler ②** (Daimler Collection; Alte Potsdamer Strasse 5; tel: 030-2594 1420; www.sammlung. daimler.com; daily 11am–6pm; free). Adjacent is the **Potsdamer-Platz-Arkaden ③** (Alte Potsdamer Strasse 7; tel: 030-255 9270; www. potsdamer-platz-arkaden.de; daily 10am–9pm), a shopping arcade.

Marlene-Dietrich-Platz

Walking south, you'll hit Marlene-Dietrich-Platz (home to **Mesa**, see ⑪③). Sights here include, at no. 1, the Musical Theater Berlin (tel: 030-259 244 555; www.stage-entertainment.de), which shows international hit musicals.

Film Festival
Each February, the area around Marlene-Dietrich-Platz turns into movie central, when the Berlinale film festival hosts Hollywood stars and newcomers alike at the Musical Theater.

Food and Drink 🍴

① LUTTER & WEGNER IM WEINHAUS HUTH
Alte Potsdamer Strasse 5; tel: 030-2529 4350; www. lutter-wegner-gendarmenmarkt.de; daily 11am–midnight; €€
Part of a chain, this bistro does light fare from Austria, France and Germany, with some hearty Berlin specialities thrown in. Excellent wine selection.

② DIEKMANN IM WEINHAUS HUTH
Alte Potsdamer Strasse 5; tel: 030-2529 7524; www.diekmann-restaurants.de; daily noon–1am; €€
This French restaurant is a favourite lunch spot for business men. In summer, the courtyard – centred around a water basin and a neon bicycle art installation by Robert Rauschenberg – is appealing.

③ MESA AT GRAND HYATT
Marlene-Dietrich-Platz 2; tel: 030-2553 1764; www.berlin.grand.hyatt.de; Sun–Thur noon–midnight; Fri/Sat noon–1am; €€
With its changing menu of tapas-style mini portions, Mesa offers the opportunity to eat yourself around the globe. The selection of wines by the bottle is superb, as is the friendly service. In summer, it's nicest to sit outside.

Above: displays at the Filmmuseum.

SONY CENTER

From here, take either Ludwig-Beck- or Varian-Fry-Strasse to the north. This brings you back to Potsdamer Platz and the **Sony Center ❹** (www. sonycenter.de), a vibrant entertainment complex, contained within a central courtyard under a glass ceiling. It was designed by the the German-American architect Helmut Jahn between 1996 and 2000 as the European headquarters for the Sony electronics giant.

In addition to shops, the complex houses the large **CineStar** (Potsdamer Strasse 4; tel: 030-2606 6400; www. cinestar.de; daily 10am–11pm; charge; *see p.120*) cinema, which shows blockbusters in their original language, and the **Filmmuseum** (Potsdamer Strasse 2; tel: 030-300 9030; www.filmmuseum-berlin. de; Tue–Sun 10am–6pm, Thur 10am–8pm; charge). The latter showcases a range of memorabilia from German cinema, including Berlin-born Marlene Dietrich's dresses and a model of the robot in *Metropolis.* One room is also dedicated to the controversial filmographer and photographer Leni Riefenstahl (1902–2003).

Adjacent to the Filmmuseum is **Billy Wilder's** bistro, see ⑪④, **Legoland** (Potsdamer Strasse 4; tel: 030-3010 4010; www.legolanddiscoverycenter. com; daily 10am–6pm; charge), although our top recommendation for a bite to eat is **Café Josty**, see ⑪⑤.

The Kaisersaal

Walk around the Josty to the right for a poignant contrast to the futuristic architecture and technological content of the Sony Center. Here you'll find the ruins (preserved behind glass walls) of the Hotel Esplanade. Before it was almost completely destroyed during World War II, the hotel was a meeting point for the international rich and famous, including stars such as Greta Garbo and Charlie Chaplin.

Continue around the building, and you'll reach the Ritz-Carlton Hotel, opposite the Sony Center. This is home to **Debrosses**, see ⑪⑥. The hotel is part of an elegant office complex, the Otto-Beisheim-Center (named after a legendary German retail entrepreneur), reminiscent of New York City's 1930s Rockefeller Centre.

KULTURFORUM

Turn around and walk down Bellevuestrasse towards the Tiergarten, then continue on Lennéstrasse and Tiergartenstrasse to the **Kulturforum ❺**, whose landmarks will be to your left. This complex of concert halls and museums was built on land levelled by both the plans of Albert Speer (Hitler's architect) to redesign the city and the bombs of World War II. It is clustered around the historic St Matthäus-Kirche *(see opposite).* The cluster of museums and cultural institutions are West Berlin's cultural gems, founded

during the 1960s as a counterpart to Museum Island *(see p.60)*, which was then in East Berlin.

Philharmonie and Kammermusiksaal

Walk down Herbert-von-Karajan-Strasse. The two tent-like buildings in the centre of the Kulturforum are the **Philharmonie** and the **Kammermusiksaal** (Herbert-von-Karajan-Strasse 1; tel: 030-254 880; www.berliner-philharmoniker.de). Designed by Hans Scharoun, they are superb examples of 1960s Modernist architecture. The Philharmonic, known for its great acoustics, is home to the Berlin Philharmonic, one of the world's most highly regarded international orchestras, with British conductor Sir Simon Rattle well established at the helm.

St Matthäus-Kirche

Opposite the Philharmonie is the **St Matthäus-Kirche ⑥** (St Matthew's Church; Matthäikirchplatz; tel: 030-262 1202; www. stiftung-stmatthaeus. de; Tue–Sun noon–6pm; free), the only historic monument on this site to have survived the devastation of the war. Built in the neo-Romanesque style in 1846 by August Stüler, it stands in dignified isolation on the square.

Gemäldegalerie

To the back of the church is the **Gemäldegalerie ⑦** (Picture Gallery; Matthäikirchplatz 4–6; tel: 030-266 3666; www.smb.museum; Tue–Sun 10am–6pm; charge). The Prussian royal family's 13th- to 18th-century holdings are displayed at this 7,000-sq m (8,370-sq yd) museum, which

Above from far left: sign for the Film-museum; illuminated Philharmonie, by Hans Scharoun.

Local Nicknames
The residents of Berlin love to give everything a nickname: not even the most high-brow of institutions are exempt. The Philharmonie's nick-name is the 'Circus Karajani' (Karajan Circus), named after revered former conductor Herbert von Karajan (1908–89).

Food and Drink

④ **BILLY WILDER'S**
Potsdamer Strasse 2; tel: 030-2655 4860; www.billywilders.de; daily 11am–2am; €
Named aafter Berlin-born movie director Billy Wilder (best known for *Some Like it Hot*), this upmarket but cosy bistro offers German and American delicatessen food, great cocktails and – particularly in the evening – an easy-going atmosphere that is popular with a young crowd. The perfect stop for a quick bite.

⑤ **CAFÉ JOSTY IM SONY CENTER**
Bellevuestrasse 1; tel: 030-2575 1105; www.josty-berlin.de; daily from 9 am; €€
This café, bar and restaurant inside the Sony Center offers a great view of the piazza from its second floor. It also has a nice little bar and some outside tables. Serves traditional Berlin dishes and some international fare.

⑥ **DEBROSSES IM RITZ-CARLTON**
Potsdamer Platz 3; tel: 030-33777; www.desbrosses.de; daily 6.30am–10.30am, 11.30am–4pm, 6–11.30pm; €€€
Debrosses is part French brasserie, part upmarket hotel restaurant. The food is a quirky but tasty mix of French and local Berlin fare. Excellent wine list.

uses ingeniously filtered natural light and special artificial light to show each of the thousand or so paintings on the main floor to its best advantage.

The art is arranged chronologically in galleries around a central atrium, with the octagonal Rembrandt room, displaying 16 of the master's works, at its apex. Particularly strong in Dutch and Flemish masters, as well as German artists, the collection at the Gemäldegalerie is the result of the painstaking reunion of works from East and West Berlin, as well as ones taken as war booty by the Soviet Union. Downstairs are an additional 400 paintings in a study collection, as well as computers connected to a digital gallery.

Decorative Arts Museum
Located nearby, on Tiergartenstrasse, is the **Kunstgewerbemuseum ❽** (Decorative Arts Museum; Tiergartenstrasse 6; tel: 030-266 2902; www.smb.museum; Tue–Fri 10am–6pm, Sat, Sun 11am–6pm; charge). The museum displays a wide range of the most exquisitely executed arts and crafts, from medieval times to the present day. Among its outstanding treasures is the Welfenschatz, comprising dazzling examples of the goldsmith's art from the 11th to the 15th centuries – richly bejewelled crosses, reliquaries and portable altars, presented to St Blasius Cathedral in Brunswick by successive generations of

Guelf (Welf) dukes. Other prized exhibits include glazed Italian majolica and a fine collection of porcelain – Chinese, Meissen, Frankenthal, Nymphenburg, as well as Berlin's own Königliche Porzellan Manufaktur (the royal KPM).

Musical Instruments Museum
Also nearby is the **Musikinstrumentenmuseum ❾** (Ben-Gurion-Strasse; tel: 030-254 810; www.sim.spk-berlin.de; Tue–Fri 9am–5pm, Sat, Sun 10am–5pm, Thur 9am–10pm; charge), designed by Hans Scharoun and reminiscent of an open card index file. Its collection of instruments from the 16th century to the present includes a 1703 Stradivarius violin, the 1810 piano of composer Carl Maria von Weber and a 1929 New York Wurlitzer cinema organ.

Neue Nationalgalerie
Now walk southwards to the **Neue Nationalgalerie ❿** (Potsdamer Strasse 50; tel: 030-266 2951; www.smb.museum; Tue–Fri 10am–6pm, Sat, Sun 11am–6pm; charge). This square, glass-walled structure with its vast, black steel roof supported by eight massive steel columns, was designed by Bauhaus master Mies van der Rohe and completed in 1968, a year before his death. The building is of characteristic elegant simplicity and considered a prime example of structural abstraction emblematic of the International

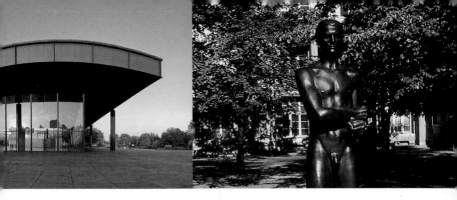

style. It stands on a raised granite platform that serves as a sculpture court for huge pieces such as Henry Moore's *Archer*.

The gallery houses an outstanding collection of 20th-century painting and sculpture, the main focus being on Cubism, Expressionism, Bauhaus and Surrealism. The development of Cubism is shown through works by Picasso, Gris, Léger and Lauens, while Expressionism is represented by some notable works by Max Beckmann as well as artists from the group Die Brücke, with works by Kirchner, Schmidt-Rottluff and Heckel. Surrealist paintings by Max Ernst, Salvador Dalí and Joan Miró are also displayed, as are New Objectivity works by Otto Dix and George Grosz.

Exponents of the Bauhaus style represented here include Kandinsky and Klee; there are also some American paintings from the 1960s and 1970s, including abstract works by Frank Stella and Ellsworth Kelly.

Note that when temporary exhibitions are on – held over long periods several times a year – the gallery's permanent collection is not on view.

RESISTANCE MEMORIAL

From the gallery, walk down Reichpietschufer to the right, with the Landwehrkanal (the canal) to your left. You will pass the 1930s Bauhaus Shell-Haus. After a few hundred metres/yards, you should turn right onto Stauffenbergstrasse.

History

The concrete complex here has always been a centre of German military command. In its earliest days it served as the headquarters of the Naval High Command of the German Empire, before becoming the German Department of War and Army High Command.

During World War II, the part of the complex known as Bendlerblock, served the Wehrmacht, the German army. It was here that a number of mostly high-ranking Prussian officers working for the Reich's home army division tried to kill Hitler on 20 July 1944 to end the war and save Germany. One of their masterminds was Colonel Claus Schenk Graf von Stauffenberg. The revolt tragically failed, and the leading men were executed that night in the courtyard here.

The Memorial

Today, the **Gedenkstätte Deutscher Widerstand** ⓫ (Memorial to the German Resistance; Stauffenbergstrasse 13–14; tel: 030-2699 5000; www.gdw-berlin.de; Mon–Wed, Fri 9am–6pm, Thur 9am–8pm, Sat, Sun 10am–6 pm; free) is Germany's central monument to these men and women. There is a museum and information centre in the former offices, which you can tour; you can also visit the courtyard in which the officers were executed.

AROUND THE BRANDENBURG GATE

The neoclassical Brandenburg Gate is one of the city's main focal points and an iconic symbol of Berlin and German history. This tour visits the gate itself and the surrounding area, home to embassies, galleries and war memorials.

DISTANCE 0.5km (⅓ mile)
TIME Half a day
START Brandenburger Tor
END Holocaust Memorial
or Wilhelmstrasse
POINTS TO NOTE
The tour is very compact, with
minimal walking involved. The
nearest station to Pariser Platz
is Unter den Linden (S-Bahn).

Right in the centre of the city, the area around the Brandenburg Gate is one of the city's most historically significant. The gate itself marks the beginning of former East Berlin. Neighbouring Wilhelmstrasse, the seat of the Prussian and Imperial German government, is now lined with government buildings. The Holocaust Memorial, visited at the end of this walk, is a sobering reminder of Germany's 20th-century history.

BRANDENBURG GATE

The **Brandenburger Tor ❶** (Brandenburg Gate) is probably the most famous monument in Germany, symbolising both the nation's triumphs and tragedies.

History
The neoclassical gate was built between 1788 and 1791 by Carl Gotthard Langhans as a triumphal arch and city gate on the road to Brandenburg. It was commissioned by King Friedrich Wilhelm as a symbol of peace, and its design was based on the Propylaea, the gateway to the Acropolis in Athens. After defeating Prussia in 1806, Napoleon took the Quadriga, the statue of a horse-drawn chariot crowning the gate, to Paris, where it remained until his defeat in the Battle of Waterloo in 1814.

During the Third Reich, the Nazis used the gate as a backdrop for their torchlight parades. The building of the Wall in 1961 left the gate in no man's land between the inner and outer border fortifications. It remained inaccessible to the public until its reopening in December 1989. Ever since, it has served as a symbol of German unity, and provides the location for one of the world's liveliest New Year's Eve parties.

Inside the Gate
The north wing of the Brandenburg Gate houses a 'quiet room', where visitors can sit and contemplate in peace; the south wing houses a Berlin Infostore (a branch of the tourist office).

PARISER PLATZ

Walk through the gate from west to east and stop on the square behind it, the broad **Pariser Platz** ❷, laid out in 1743. On your left, on the northern side, you'll see the **Französische Botschaft** (French Embassy), at no. 5 in the northeastern corner. Nearby, at no. 6a, is **Café Theodor Tucher**, see ⓕ①, a good place for breakfast or lunch.

In the same corner is **The Kennedys** ❸ (Pariser Platz 4a; tel: 030-2065 3570; www.thekennedys.de; daily 10am–6pm; charge), which houses a collection of photographs, documents and memorabilia related to the family of the former US President. It commemorates JFK's 1963 visit to the divided city, when he erroneously declared, 'Ich bin ein Berliner' (which, amusingly, can mean 'I am a doughnut').

Southern Side

On the opposite side of the square (the right-hand side with the gate behind you) is the **US Embassy** (closed to the public), opened in 2008 at no. 2. At no. 3 is the **DZ Bank** ❹, designed in 2000 by the Canadian-born architect Frank Gehry. Inside is a remarkable atrium covered by a vaulted glass roof said to have the form of a fish; beneath this a walk-in sculpture resembling Captain Nemo's *Nautilus* (actually the outer skin of a conference room). Visitors can pop in, but only as far as the security turnstiles.

Adjacent is the new home of the **Akademie der Künste** ❺ (Academy of Arts; Pariser Platz 4; tel: 030-200 570; www.adk.de; Tue–Fri 11am–8pm; charge), a contemporary building with a glass façade by Günter Behnisch. It integrates the historic ruins of the Berlin

Above: the iconic Brandenburg Gate.

Food and Drink

① CAFÉ THEODOR TUCHER
Pariser Platz 6a; tel: 030-2248 9464; www.thementeam.de; daily 9am–1am; €€
This bookish café offers nice views of the Pariser Platz and, in summer, has some great outdoor tables. The food ranges from light bistro dishes to hearty mains to rich German cakes.

② CAFÉ AKADEMIE DER KÜNSTE PARISER PLATZ
Sarah Wiener's, Pariser Platz 4; tel: 030-2005 71723; www.sarahwiener.de; daily 10am–6pm; €
The café at the rear of the Academy is popular with culture buffs and is known for its delicious, strong German coffee. The menu includes pastries and light international dishes.

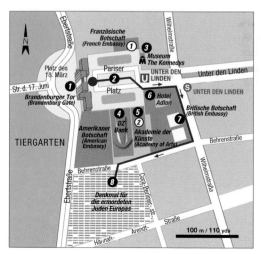

Academy of Arts. Inside, exhibits, lectures and more attract culture buffs. The café here, see ⑪②, p.51, is worth a stop.

HOTEL ADLON

The southeastern corner of the Pariser Platz is dominated by one of the city's most prestigious hotels, the massive **Hotel Adlon ❻** (Unter den Linden 77; tel: 030-22610; www.hotel-adlon.de). The current building is a 1997 replica of a historic hotel that occupied this spot until World War II. The East German Socialist regime demolished what remained of the building after the war, and the site remained empty until the fall of the Wall. More than a decade after its renovation, the Adlon is popular with officials, including the last four US Presidents, and celebrities from film stars to musicians.

BRITISH EMBASSY

Walking south onto Wilhelmstrasse you'll see a large Union flag, which marks the **Britische Botschaft ❼** (British Embassy; Wilhelmstrasse 70; tel: 030-204 570; ukingermany.fco.gov. uk; Mon–Fri 9am–5.30pm) on the left. This is Britain's only embassy to have been opened by Queen Elizabeth II.

Below: the main hall of the Gehry-designed DZ Bank *(see p.51).*

HOLOCAUST MEMORIAL

Continue south down Wilhelmstrasse and take the first right – Behrenstrasse. Here, you can't miss the field of dark grey stone monoliths, the **Denkmal für die ermordeten Juden Europas** ❽ (Cora-Berliner-Strasse 1; tel: 030-200 7660; www.stiftung-denkmal.de; daily 10am–8pm; free), also known as the Holocaust Memorial.

The project to build a memorial to the Jews massacred during Hitler's reign proved controversial – it was first planned in 1988–9 but was the subject of great debate until New York architect Peter Eisenmann's design was chosen and realised in 2003. It was not only the minimalist design that came under fire, but also the possible inclusion of non-Jewish victims of the Nazis, such as men and women of other ethnicities, homosexuals, Sinti and Roma and resistance fighters.

Opened in December 2004, the memorial consists of a 1.9ha (4¾-acre) site, covered with a grid of 2,700 blank concrete stelae, intended to inspire visitors to reflect on the Holocaust and its victims. The information centre underground chronicles the ideology and history of the genocide and shows the names of all known Jewish victims.

Note that sitting or climbing on the stones is not allowed, both for safety reasons and in reverence to the memorial's significance. You can, however, walk between them, and take pictures.

NAZI HEADQUARTERS

While here, it's worth considering that this area – traditionally the location for German state buildings – was once home to the Nazis' headquarters. If you want to explore a little further, head back to Wilhelmstrasse by following Behrenstrasse east, then turning right. This was the location for Hitler's Neue Reichskanzlei (New Chancellery), designed and built in the Fascist style by the Führer's chief architect, Albert Speer, in just one year (1936). The New Chancellery was destroyed at the end of the war, with its ruins later completely demolished. The site on which it once stood is now replaced by 1980s Socialist apartment buildings.

Hitler's Bunker

Within the New Chancellery was the Führerbunker (Hitler's Bunker), where Hitler spent the last weeks of the war and committed suicide on 30 April 1945. A playground marks the spot under which it was previously located. Despite what the tour guides claim, there is nothing left of this bunker, which was blown up several times; only the base foundation remains, and this is several metres underground. Well-preserved bunkers have, however, been found nearby in the years since the war – these were used by drivers and guards of the Chancellery, but have been sealed, with their locations kept secret, in order to avoid attention from neo-Nazis.

Above from far left: Holocaust Memorial.

Below: Hotel Adlon

Nazi Interiors
Although Hitler's New Chancellery was completed demolished, some of its lavish interiors nevertheless found their way into buildings across Berlin. The dark-red marble from the long halls was later reused at Mohrenstrasse U-Bahn station, in the lobby of the Humboldt University (see p.56) and in the Russian Embassy (see p.54) on Unter den Linden.

UNTER DEN LINDEN TO ALEXANDERPLATZ

Unter den Linden is Berlin's grand old boulevard, lined with historic buildings and monuments. Beyond it, to the east, is Alexanderplatz, flattened in World War II but now home to landmarks including the Fernsehturm.

DISTANCE	6.5km (4 miles)
TIME	A full day
START	Pariser Platz
END	Alexanderplatz

POINTS TO NOTE

This tour is long and can be divided into two sections: a walk down Unter den Linden, then a tour of the Nikolaiviertel and Alexanderplatz. To reach the starting point of the main tour by public transport, take the S-Bahn to Unter den Linden station. Watch out for busy traffic when crossing Unter den Linden.

Above: statue of Frederick the Great; Berliner Dom; the Fernsehturm.

First laid out as a riding path between the City Palace and the Tiergarten hunting grounds in the 16th century, Unter den Linden quickly evolved as the Prussian, then the Imperial capital's central thoroughfare during the mid-17th century, making it social, cultural and political centre of Berlin. The name comes from the lime trees planted along the avenue – the trees survived the heavy bombing suffered here in World War II.

AROUND PARISER PLATZ

Start your walk down Unter den Linden at the **Pariser Platz** ❶ *(see p.51)*, and head east along the boulevard on its southern side. Many of the buildings at the start of the street here are offices for German members of parliament and international government authorities. The first of these, at nos 63–5, is the **Botschaft Russische Föderation** ❷ (Russian Embassy), built in the 1950s and a good example of Stalinist architecture. Note the window in the middle showing a rainbow rising above the Kremlin – the promise of a bright future (the vision when the embassy was built). A bronze bust of the founder of that vision, Lenin, has, however, long been removed from the front garden.

Before crossing Glinkastrasse, note that the **Café Einstein**, see ⑪①, is located just opposite.

Komische Oper

Back on the southern side of the avenue, you'll reach the **Komische Oper Berlin** ❸ (Behrenstrasse 55–7; tel: 030-4799 7400; www.komische-oper-berlin.de),

set back from Unter den Linden slightly. The unprepossessing modern façade is the result of post-war reconstruction; fortunately, the magnificently over-the-top gilded interior has been retained. Light operatic works in German (and German translation), including operettas and operatic pieces for children, are performed here.

Deutsche Guggenheim

Heading east again, just after Charlottenstrasse, on the right, is the **Deutsche Guggenheim Berlin** ❹ (Unter den Linden 13–15; tel: 030-202 0930; www. deutsche-guggenheim-berlin.de; daily 10am–8pm, Thur 10am–10pm; charge except Mon), which puts on changing modern and contemporary art shows. Don't expect exhibitions on the scale of the New York or Bilbao Guggenheims, however, or you'll be disappointed – this branch is small, and there are only a few rooms of works. The café and shop at the back are nice, though.

Historic Libraries

Back on the northern side of Unter den Linden, you'll pass the **Staatsbibliothek** ❺ (Unter den Linden 8; tel: 030-2660; http://staatsbibliothek-berlin.de; Mon–Fri 9am–9pm, Sat 9am–7pm; free), the old state library. Opposite is the Baroque **Alte Bibliothek** ❻ (Unter den Linden 11), the historic city library, whose curved profile has led to it being given the rather unfortunate nickname of the 'Kommode' (commode).

In the middle of the street, just by the Alte Bibliothek, note the bronze sculpture of the Prussian king Frederick the Great *(see p. 92)*, riding high and proud. Legend has it that the East German regime turned the statue around, so that Frederick faced east, but historic records show that he has always been riding down the Linden facing that way.

FORUM FRIDERICIANUM

One of the Frederick's lasting achievements, in line with his idea of enlightenment, is embodied opposite his sculpture, in the **Forum Fridericianum**, the fine neoclassical and Baroque buildings clustered around Bebelplatz (formerly Opernplatz).

Staatsoper

The forum includes the **Staatsoper** ❼ (Unter den Linden 7; tel: 030-2035 4438; www.staatsoper-berlin.org; tours available in German – days change per week, so check website for details; pre-arranged group tours in English also offered; charge for tours), built by Georg Wenzeslaus von Knobelsdorff

---

Food and Drink 🍴

① CAFÉ EINSTEIN
Unter den Linden 42; tel: 030-204 3632; www.einsteinudl. com; Mon–Sun 7am–10pm; €€
This restaurant is one of the nicest on Unter den Linden and is popular with both an arty and a political crowd. Serves traditional Austrian dishes such as a thin and ultra-crispy Wiener schnitzel as well as more rustic Berlin specialities.

Above from left: Humboldt-Universität; the area by night.

Humboldt-Forum
Heavy reconstruction work is currently going on on the site once occupied by the Palace of the Republic. Scheduled for completion by 2013, the Humboldt-Forum by Italian architect Francesco Stella will be a cultural/museum complex, and will incorporate some of the old façade of the Hohezollern Palace.

in 1741–3. This was the world's first free-standing opera house, ie the first not part of a palace. The repertoire focusses on classical opera and ballet. The interior is worth a look and can be visited on a tour, although note that the building will undergo restoration in 2010, so check the website for updates. In the adjacent **Opernpalais** is the **Operncafé**, see ⑪②.

St Hedwigskathedrale
Walk across the square to the **St Hedwigskathedrale** ❽ (Bebelplatz; tel: 030-203 4810; www.hedwigs-kathedrale.de; daily 10am–6pm; free). The oddly shaped cathedral, built in 1747 just after the Reformation, is the city's leading Catholic place of worship. The interior was badly damaged during World War II, and the replacement is minimalist and sober.

HUMBOLDT UNIVERSITY TO MUSEUM ISLAND

Now walk back onto Unter den Linden, where, on the northern side of the road, is the **Humboldt-Universität** ❾ (HU; Unter den Linden 6; tel: 030-20930; www.hu-berlin.de; Mon–Fri 6am–10pm, Sat 10am–6pm), one of the country's most esteemed seats of learning. The university was founded in 1810, but cast into the shadows somewhat during the Nazi regime – many of the writers banned by the Nazis had been teaching or studying at the HU – and the following 40 years of Socialist rule. Pop into the lobby to see its dark-red marble cladding, taken from Hitler's destroyed Chancellery *(see p.53)*. Outside the building, browse the second-hand book stands that are a regular feature here.

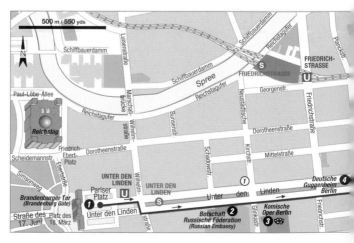

Neue Wache

Continue walking east on the northern side of Under den Linden to no. 4, home of the **Neue Wache** ⑩ (daily 10am–6pm; free). This small building, resembling a temple with its columns and simple portico, was once a guard-house but is now the country's central memorial to victims of war and tyranny. Inside, note the replica of a *Pietà* by the artist Käthe Kollwitz *(see p.35 and 86).*

Deutsches Historisches Museum

Just a few steps away is the huge pink-fronted Baroque **Zeughaus** (Arsenal), built from 1695 to 1730 for the Prussian armoury. Since 1952 it has housed the **Deutsches Historisches Museum** ⑪ (Unter den Linden 2; tel: 030-2030 4444; www.dhm.de; daily 10am–6pm; charge), showcasing German history from the Middle Ages to the present

day. The inner courtyard is worth a peek for its smart glass roof and for its *Dying Warriors*, stone sculptures by Andreas Schlüter, one of the leading sculptors of the Baroque period. The Zeughaus also shows historical films and has an inviting café.

Royal Residences

To the left of the Zeughaus are two buildings forming the neoclassical **Kronprinzenpalais** ⑫ (Palace of the Crown Prince and Princesses; Unter

Prize Winners

Great minds such as Hegel, Fichte, Einstein, Planck and Marx have left their mark at the Humboldt University, making this the German university with the highest number of Nobel Prize winners. To date, the total is 30.

Food and Drink 🍴

② OPERNCAFÉ IM OPERNPALAIS
Unter den Linden 5; tel: 030-202 683; www.opernpalais.de;
8am–midnight; €€
This café is a renovated version of an old-style German coffeehouse, serving a big selection of freshly baked tarts and pastries. In the morning it also does hearty breakfasts. Expect queues on weekend afternoons.

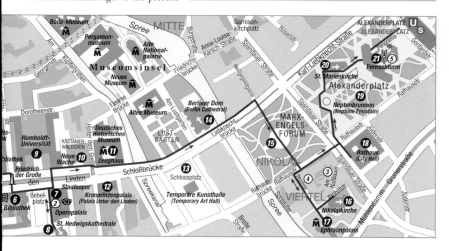

Above: statue in the Nikolaiviertel.

Berlin Alexanderplatz

The German writer Alfred Döblin set his 1929 novel in 1920s Berlin, in the working-class district around Alexanderplatz. His anti-hero, Franz Biberkopf, is fresh out of prison, determined to stay clean. Inevitably, perhaps, he gets sucked into the Berlin criminal underbelly, and trouble ensues. The novel was made into a film in 1931 and, more famously, in 1980, into a 14-part, 15.5-hour television series directed by Rainer Werner Fassbender and starring Günter Lamprecht (Biberkopf) and Elisabeth Trissenaar.

den Linden 3; tel: 030-203 040; Mon, Tue, Fri–Sun 10am–6pm, Thur 10am–10pm; free), once the living quarters of the young Hohenzollern princes and princesses. The palace now serves as a venue for events and exhibitions.

MUSEUM ISLAND

You have now reached the culturally rich **Museumsinsel** (Museum Island), a Unesco-protected area that incorporates the Pergamonmuseum, the Bode-Museum, the Altes Museum, the Neues Museum and the Alte National-galerie, covered in full on walk 6 *(see p.60)*. If you have time, go into one or several of these. Alternatively, continue walking, crossing the Schlossbrücke, decorated with fine sculptures.

On your right is **Schlossplatz** ⓭, which was heavily bombed in World War II. It is now the slightly incongruous location for the **Temporäre Kunsthalle** (Temporary Art Hall; Schlossfreiheit 1; tel: 030-2576 2040; www.kunsthalle-berlin.com; Mon 11am–10pm, Tue–Sun 11am–6pm; charge), a makeshift blue-and-white cube that is used as a showcase for contemporary art. Behind it is a large open space that was once the location of the Hohenzollern City Palace and, later, for that of the East German parliament (in the Palace of the Republic), the East German Foreign Ministry and, on the southern side, the Staatsratsgebäude (the State Council Building). Only the

Staatsratsgebäude remains, although rather ironically it now serves a private business school.

BERLINER DOM

On your left you'll soon pass the **Berliner Dom** ⓮ (Berlin Cathedral; Am Lustgarten; tel: 030-2026 9119; www.berlinerdom.de; Apr–Sept: Mon–Sat 9am–8pm, Sun noon–8pm, Oct–Mar: Mon–Sat 9am–7pm, Sun noon–7pm; charge), the largest Protestant church in Berlin. Built on the site of an older church, the current, well-restored edifice dates to 1894–1905. It was designed by Julius Raschdorff as the central Imperial church of the Hohenzollerns. Highlights of a visit include the main hall with its royal sarcophagi, the neo-Baroque pulpit, the Imperial Staircase, clad in elegant black marble, and the huge crypt with further royal graves.

NIKOLAIVIERTEL

Now turn into the park to your right. This pleasant little area is the **Marx-Engels-Forum** ⓯, embellished with sculptures of the two eponymous philosophers. Continue walking south and cross Rathausstrasse into the maze of streets inside the Nikolaiviertel (Nicholas Quarter). Although heavily restored, with many replica buildings (and more than its fair share of tourists), this is the oldest and most historic part

of town, and it gives a good impression of what late 17th-century Berlin would have looked like. Key sights include the city's oldest church, the original **Nikolaikirche** ⑯ (St Nicholas's Church; Nikolaikirchplatz; tel: 030-2400 2162; www.stadtmuseum.de; free), as well as the façade of the Baroque **Ephraimpalais** ⑰ (Poststrasse 16; tel: 030-2400 2121; www.stadtmuseum.de; Tue–Sun 10am–6pm, Wed noon–8pm; charge), just a few steps away. Food stops include **Zum Nussbaum** and **Reinhards**, see ⑪③ and ⑪④.

Town Hall

Walk back through Poststrasse onto Rathausstrasse, then take a right towards the huge red building in front of you. This is the **Rathaus** ⑱ (City Hall; Rathausstrasse 15; tel: 030-9026 3001; www.berlin.de; daily 8am–6pm). Nicknamed 'red city hall', it was built in 1861–9 as a symbol of the then newly proclaimed Imperial capital. It owes its name to the red stones used in its construction and not – as many think – from any political affiliations, even though Berlin has been governed by a left-wing coalition for quite some time now. The offices of the Mayor can be seen on the second floor to the left of the clock tower.

ALEXANDERPLATZ

Ahead of you at this point is **Alexanderplatz** ⑲, once one of the city's great squares but almost completely flattened in World War II. Highlights include the **Neptunbrunnen** (Neptune Fountain) and, behind it, the **Marienkirche** ⑳ (Karl-Liebknecht-Strasse 8; tel: 030-242 4467; www.marienkirche-berlin.de; daily: Apr–Sept 10am–9pm, Oct–Mar 10am–6pm; free).

Fernsehturm

If you have not yet seen enough of the Berlin skyline, take the ride up the **Fernsehturm** ㉑ (Panoramastrasse 1a; tel: 030-242 3333; www.berlinerfernsehturm.de; daily 9am–midnight), Berlin's television tower, whose revolving café, see ⑪⑤, offers impressive views of Berlin and the surrounding countryside.

Above from far left: cupola of the Berliner Dom; Alexanderplatz and Fernsehturm.

Food and Drink ⑪

③ ZUM NUSSBAUM
Am Nussbaum 3; tel: 030-242 3095; daily noon–2am; €
This quirky little joint in the Nikolaiviertel is one of Berlin's most authentic pubs, with a restaurant focusing on simple but tasty local dishes and good beer. Convivial atmosphere.

④ REINHARDS
Poststrasse 28; tel: 030-242 5295; www.reinhards.de; daily 9am–midnight; €€
This upmarket old-style restaurant evokes the 1920s with its interior, the music and the hearty traditional Berlin dishes such as liver with baked apples, onions and mashed potatoes.

⑤ TELECAFÉ IM FERNSEHTURM
Panoramastrasse 1a; tel: 030-242 3333; www.berliner fernsehturm.de; daily 9am–midnight; €
The Telecafé offers light dishes and cakes, which are tasty but not outstanding. Most guests come here for the view, enjoying the slowly rotating café for a 360-degree panoramic view of the city.

MUSEUM ISLAND

The focus of this tour is the culturally rich Museumsinsel (Museum Island), located between the River Spree and the Spree Canal at the eastern end of Unter den Linden, still within the Mitte district. The Unesco-protected island is home to a cluster of museums of international cultural importance.

Above: statues in the Pergamonmuseum.

Tickets

The collections on Museum Island are part of Berlin's State Museum system and can be visited by buying a combined ticket for €14, for one day. A three-day ticket (€19) is also valid for state museums here and at the Kulturforum *(see p.46)*. Each Thursday night, the museums are open late until 10pm; entrance is also free on Thursday evenings.

DISTANCE 2km (1¼ miles)

TIME A full day

START Pergamonmuseum

END Berliner Dom

POINTS TO NOTE

Note that most of the museums on Museum Island get very crowded at the weekend. Restaurant options are quoted together on this tour, *see opposite*. Picnicking is a good option here *(see box opposite)*. All the museums open late on Thursdays, when it's free to get in. The easiest way to reach the area by public transport is by taking the S-Bahn to Friedrichstrasse or Hackescher Markt or by taking bus no. 100 or 200 along Unter den Linden to the Schlossbrücke. The tour distance quoted above does not include ground covered within the museums themselves.

Museumsinsel (Museum Island) takes up the northern half of the Spree Island, defined by the River Spree to the northeast and the Spree Canal to the southwest. It is home to five museums of international importance, most of which were built between 1912 and 1930. The southern part of the Spree Island, Fischerinsel (Fishermen's Island, named after the fishermen who once lived and worked here), forms the cradle of Berlin, where the medieval city came into existence, although it is now dominated by rather depressing tower blocks.

Only a fraction of the full collections is on show, but even so it would take days to see everything on display in each museum. At a relatively speedy pace, you could, however, see the highlights of each museum on the island in a day, as described here. Note that many of the labels accompanying the exhibits in the museums are in German only, but English-language audio guides are available at all the museums.

PERGAMONMUSEUM

The tour starts at the **Pergamonmuseum ❶** (Am Kupfergraben 5; tel: 030-2090 5577; www.smb.museum; daily 10am–6pm, Thur 10am–10pm; charge), accessed across a bridge over the Kupfergraben Canal.

A major reconstruction of this museum commenced in 2008, and while parts of it will be closed, the museum will remain open.

The Collection

With over a million visitors annually, this is one of Germany's most popular museums, and with good reason: what other museum can boast not only an entire Greek temple complex, but also the approach to the city of Babylon and its fabled Ishtar Gate?

The Pergamon temple complex was excavated by Carl Umann in 1864–5 with the cooperation of the Turkish government and moved, stone by stone, to this museum, built specially to house it. The frieze showing a battle between the Greek gods and the Giants is one of Hellenic art's masterpieces.

Other pieces of Classical sculpture can be seen in the wings off the central temple room. The ancient Near Eastern collection is just as impressive, not only because of the Babylonian walls, but the Desert Palace of Mshatta from Jordan. In addition, the Museum of Islamic Art is upstairs and forms a small but inclusive survey of the subject, including the impressive Aleppo Room from the Syrian city's Christian quarter.

BODE-MUSEUM

Next stop is the **Bode-Museum** ❷ (Monbijoubrücke; tel: 030-2090 5577;

www.smb.museum; Mon–Wed, Fri–Sun 10am–6pm, Thur 10am–10pm; charge), accessed by going back over the canal, then crossing Monbijoubrücke.

The Collection

The Bode-Museum's church-like interior, which maximises light and space, makes it a stunning venue for the medieval and Renaissance sculpture collection, which includes wooden

Food and Drink

All of the cafés and bistros on Museum Island offer affordable coffee, good cakes and pastries as well as light sandwiches and other quick bites. Though some of these are not very flashy or outright inviting, they are nevertheless the only option for a break on the island itself. In summer, the street vendors outside may be a better choice. Alternatively, buy a picnic and do as the Berliners do by lounging on the meadows of the Lustgarten in front of the Altes Museum.

① CAFÉ IM PERGAMONMUSEUM
Am Kupfergraben 5; tel: 030-2090 6361; www.smb.museum; Mon–Wed and Fri–Sun 10am–6pm, Thur 10am–10pm; €

② CAFÉ IM BODE-MUSEUM
Monbijoubrücke; tel: 030-2021 4330; www.smb.museum; Mon–Wed and Fri–Sun 10am–6pm, Thur 10am–10pm; €

③ CAFÉ IM NEUES MUSEUM
Closed until late 2009. See www.smb.museum for up-to-date information on opening and facilities.

④ CAFÉ IM ALTE NATIONALGALERIE
Bodestrase 1–3; tel: 030-2064 9043; www.smb.museum; Mon–Wed and Fri–Sun 10am–6pm, Thur 10am–10pm; €

⑤ CAFÉ IM ALTES MUSEUM
Am Lustgarten; tel: 030-2090 5251; www.smb.museum; Mon–Wed and Fri–Sun 10am–6pm, Thur 10am–10pm; €

carving masterpieces by Erasmus Grasser and Tilman Riemenschneider. There are also French, Dutch, Spanish and Italian works from this period and sculptures from the Baroque and Romantic periods. The Byzantine collection has many early Christian works, including carved ivory devotional items and an impressive mosaic chapel.

Other highlights here are the Basilica, a great hall in which altarpieces from European churches are displayed with paintings appropriate to the period, and the Numismatic Collection, one of the best collections of coins in the world.

NEUES MUSEUM

Leaving the Bode-Museum, walk back south along Am Kupfergraben, passing the Pergamonmuseum. Turn left onto the Eiserne Brücke and on your left you will see the **Neues Museum** ❸ (Bodestrasse 1–3; tel: 030-2090 5577; www.smb.museum). Opened in autumn 2009 after restoration, it showcases the Egyptian Museum's collection and parts of the museum for pre- and early history. Its star attractions include a bust of the Egyptian queen Nefertiti, admired for its hypnotic smile and elegant curve of the neck.

Below: the Bode-Museum.

ALTE NATIONALGALERIE

Next stop is the neoclassical **Alte Nationalgalerie ❹** (Bodestrasse 1–3; tel: 030-2090 5577; www.smb.museum; Mon–Wed and Fri–Sun 10am–6pm, Thur 10am–10pm; charge), just behind the Neues Museum, although hidden somewhat behind a colonnade. The gallery houses the Berlin National Museums' massive collection of 19th-century art under one roof. The third floor displays entirely German painters, including masterpieces by Caspar David Friedrich, as well as architectural renderings by Karl Friedrich Schinkel.

On the second floor, a large number of French Impressionists, including Manet, Monet and Renoir, are joined by their German contemporaries, including Feuerbach, Böcklin and Liebermann. The first floor has a display of Adolf Menzel's paintings and an extensive collection of 19th-century German sculpture.

ALTES MUSEUM

From the Nationalgalerie take Am Lustgarten, a narrow street heading south. On your right you will pass the Berliner Dom, while on your left you'll see the **Altes Museum ❺** (Am Lustgarten; tel: 030-2090 5577; www.smb. museum; Mon–Wed, Fri–Sun 10am–6pm, Thur 10am–10pm; charge). Walk all the way to the end of the street, then approach the museum through the Lustgarten park in front of it. This is the best way to take the fine symmetric design of the neoclassical building, designed by Karl Friedrich Schinkel in 1823–30. The museum showcases a large number of Greek antiquities – mostly vases, sculptures, coins, jewellery and other artefacts – complementing the Greek collection housed in the Pergamonmuseum (see p.61).

BERLINER DOM

If you have time, finish your tour of Museum Island with a visit to the **Berliner Dom ❻** (Berlin Cathedral; Am Lustgarten; tel: 030-2026 9119; www.berlinerdom.de; Apr–Sept: Mon–Sat 9am–8pm, Sun noon–8pm, Oct–Mar: Mon–Sat 9am–7pm, Sun noon–7pm; charge), the largest Protestant church in Berlin (see p.58).

Above from far left: admiring the artworks at the Alte Nationalgalerie; sculpture on the exterior of the Alte Nationalgalerie.

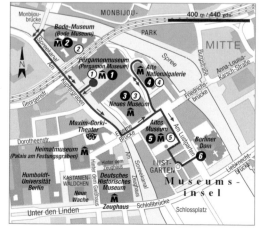

SCHEUNENVIERTEL

The district explored on this walk forms the northern section of Mitte − the area running east along the north bank of the Spree from Friedrichstrasse to Hackescher Markt. From its early days as an out-of-town hay store, Scheunenviertel has evolved into one of the funkiest parts of the capital.

DISTANCE 3km (2 miles)
TIME Half a day
START Hackescher Höfe
END Kunst-Werke
POINTS TO NOTE

All attractions on this tour are within easy walking distance. If you need to get to the starting point by public transport, take the S-Bahn to Hackescher Markt. Note that this area gets packed at the weekends.

Food and Drink

① **HACKESCHER HOF**
Rosenthaler Strasse 40–1; tel: 030-283 5293; www.hackescherhof.gs-domain.de; Mon–Fri 7am–1am, Sat–Sun 9am–1am; €€
With its high ceiling, dark wooden furniture, starched white linen and friendly service, the Hackescher Hof is a traditional Berlin-style restaurant serving great local and international food. In summer, try to get a table in the courtyard.

② **OXYMORON**
Rosenthaler Strasse 40–1; tel: 030-2839 1886; www.oxymoron-berlin.de; Nov–Apr 10am–late; May–Oct 9am–late; €€
The quirky but classy Oxymoron is a bar with bistro and restaurant, offering some of the best tables in the Hackescher Höfe for people-watching. The light, international menu is tasty, as are the 80 or so cocktails on offer.

When talking about 'Mitte', most people in Berlin think of this area, its northern part. Scheunenviertel (literally Barn Quarter) was once far enough away from the city centre for flammable hay barns to be built here. In its earliest days it was a poor quarter for craftsmen, but in the late 19th century, it (and the adjacent Spandauer Vorstadt − typically lumped in as one with Scheunenviertel) became the home to the city's largest Jewish community − many members of which were fleeing persecution in Russia and Eastern Europe.

After the devastation of the Nazi period, the area went into heavy decline. In the 1990s, low rents began to attract artists and bohemians, and, as a result, the area has evolved as one of the artiest in the city. Things are upmarket bohemian here nowadays, with a proliferation of cool fashion boutiques, trendy art galleries and lots of bars, cafés and restaurants.

HACKESCHER MARKT

The western end of the district is marked by the S-Bahn station Hack-

escher Markt. The square of the same name is a busy spot, popular with visitors and locals alike, and with street artists entertaining the masses. Trams compete for space with tour buses and cyclists in the narrow lanes in this area. The railway tracks are elevated here, and the red-brick arches beneath them house a number of cafés and restaurants.

Hackesche Höfe

Head for the **Hackesche Höfe** ❶ (Rosenthaler Strasse 40–1 and Sophienstrasse 6; www.hackesche-hoefe.com), located just opposite the station. Typical for Mitte, this warehouse complex of nine interconnected courtyards, dating to 1905–7 and built by Jewish idealists, has been meticulously restored. This by far the largest and most beautiful of the many such complexes in this area. Elements of the Jugendstil (the German and Austrian form of Art Nouveau) style are most visible in the first courtyard; note the glazed blue-and-white tiles and the mosaics. There are a couple of pleasant cafés here: **Hackescher Hof** and **Café Oxymoron**, see ⑪① and ⑪②.

The complex also houses the 1906 **Varieté Chamäleon** (www.chamaeleon berlin.de; *see p.120*), a renovated Jugendstil theatre and music and cabaret hall, with a restored ballroom as well as the architecture café and gallery Aedes and numerous fashion boutiques. Take time out to explore all the courtyards – as you get further through, they become

increasingly peaceful, peppered with fountains and trees.

SOPHIENSTRASSE

When leaving the Hackesche Höfe through the last courtyard, you'll emerge onto Sophienstrasse, one of the neighbourhood's most attractive alleys, dotted with craft workshops, from instrument makers to art galleries. These workshops have been restored in the style of ateliers located here in the 18th century, when the street was first laid out.

Follow Sophienstrasse down to your left, past a red-brick gateway hiding a small courtyard, the **Sophienhöfe**, (Sophienstrasse 17–18), once used by the Singer sewing-machine manufacturer. A few steps further up, at nos 21–2, are the **Sophie-Gips-Höfe**, housing one of Berlin's premier modern art galleries, the Galerie Hoffmann (tours available on Sat, by prior arrangement only).

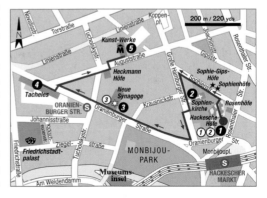

Above: Star of David and dome, both at the Neue Synagogue.

Moses Mendelssohn
Look out, on Grosse Hamburger Strasse, for a memorial marking what is thought to be the grave of the German Jewish philosopher Moses Mendelssohn (1729–86), one of Germany's most famous thinkers of the Jewish Enlightenment and the founder of the city's first Jewish School.

GROSSE HAMBURGER STRASSE

At the end of the street, you will pass a graveyard hidden behind a church, the Baroque **Sophienkirche** ❷ (Grosse Hamburger Strasse 29; tel: 030-308 7920; www.sophien.de; May–Sept Wed 3–6pm, Sat 3–5pm), after which Sophienstrasse is named. Built in 1712, this was the first Protestant church in a predominantly Jewish area. To admire the front, you have to walk left from Sophienstrasse onto Grosse Hamburger Strasse.

Jewish School
Grosse Hamburger Strasse was once the centre of Jewish life in this area (a part of the district known as the Spandauer Vorstadt – actually separate from Scheunenviertel – located on and west of Oranienburger Strasse). After a few steps, you'll pass, at no. 27, a nondescript white building on your right; this was once a Jewish school (and also at one time a hospital). In 1941, the Nazis turned the school into a central 'assembly' office for the 50,000 Jews still in the ghetto at that time, deporting them to concentration camps from here. A memorial commemorates the fact. A low wall behind the memorial hides what little is left of an old Jewish cemetery destroyed by the Nazis.

Of the more than 160,000 Jews living in Berlin in the early 1930, only 5,000 survived the Holocaust, some hidden by Berlin families. Today, the city's Jewish community, mostly living in Mitte and Charlottenburg, is estimated at 20,000 – and Jewish life is thriving again in Berlin, thanks to the influx of Jewish families from the Commonwealth of Independent States (CIS) since 1990.

ORANIENBURGER STRASSE

At the end of Grosse Hamburger Strasse, turn right onto Oranienburger Strasse. Thanks to the many cafés and restaurants lining this wide street, it has become another nightlife hub (although also something of a red-light area).

Neue Synagoge
Oranienburger Strasse is also one of the focal points of the Jewish Quarter and the location of the **Neue Synagoge** ❸ (Oranienburger Strasse 28–30; tel: 030-8802 8300; www.cjudaicum.de), recognisable by its splendid golden dome. Built between 1859 and 1866 by the Berlin architect Eduard Knobloch, the synagogue was inspired by the Alhambra in Granada, southern Spain, and was at one time the largest on the European continent, with room for more than 3,000 worshippers.

The synagogue was attacked on Kristallnacht (9 November 1938) but did not burn down, in large part due to the courage of police officer Wilhelm Krützfeld, who stopped the looting.

A small plaque on the temple's façade honours the man.

The main temple was, however, destroyed by Allied bombs in 1943, and a modern centre for Jewish culture and religion, the Centrum Judaicum, has been built in its place. Here, you can indulge in Jewish and Middle Eastern food, at **Kadima**, see ⑪③.

Tacheles

Continuing on Oranienburger Strasse, you will soon see an odd-looking ruin, the remains of the **Tacheles** ❹ (Oranienburger Strasse 54–6a; tel: 030-282 6185; http://super.tacheles.de/; daily 24 hours; free), a large, elegant shopping complex devastated during the war and unrestored thereafter. Following the fall of the Wall, artists moved in, squatting and working here. In the late 1990s, the building was bought by a developer, who has renovated much of the building, setting up galleries. You can watch artists in progress, and attend art events that run in the evenings.

AUGUSTSTRASSE

Retrace your tracks slightly along Oranienburgerstrasse, then turn left into Auguststrasse, which runs northeast. The unofficial art alley of Berlin – sometimes dubbed Mitte's 'Art Mile' – this enticing long, narrow strip is home to a concentration of art, design and photography galleries. Take time out to explore them, and try to drop by the **Heckmann Höfe** (Auguststrasse 9; www.heckmann-hoefe.de), a small, attractive courtyard complex. Many of the area's most cutting-edge galleries have moved on, but there is still much here to keep art buffs happy.

Kunst-Werke

A big highlight is located just a few steps further up the street, in the galleries at the Baroque **Kunst-Werke** ❺ (Auguststrasse 69; tel: 030-243 4590; www.kw-berlin.de; Tue–Sun noon–7pm, Thur noon–9pm; charge), a former factory that is now Mitte's main art and events centre, showcasing contemporary artists on a non-profit basis.

From here, if you turn right onto Grosse Hamburger Strasse, this will take you back to the **Hackescher Höfe**, where you started.

Food and Drink ⑪

③ KADIMA

Oranienburger Strasse 28; tel; 030-2759 4251; www.kadima-restaurant.com; Mon–Sat 5pm–midnight, Sun noon–midnight; €€

This pleasant restaurant serves a mix of traditional Jewish and more exotic Middle Eastern delicacies – 'Kadima' is Hebrew for 'forward', and the cuisine is correspondingly creatively advanced. The good wine list and the friendly service make this one of the best dinner choices in the neighbourhood.

FRIEDRICHSTRASSE AND GENDARMENMARKT

This tour explores Friedrichstrasse, one of Berlin's grand old thoroughfares, and, at its southern end, Karl Friedrich Schinkel's architecturally harmonious Gendarmenmarkt complex, comprising the Konzerthaus Berlin, the Deutscher Dom and the Französischer Dom.

Art Bunker
On Reinhardstrasse, look out for one of Berlin's last remaining Hochbunker (a bunker built on the surface). It now doubles as an art gallery.

DISTANCE 3km (2 miles)
TIME A full day
START S-Bahnhof Friedrichstrasse
END Museum für Kommunikation
POINTS TO NOTE
This tour starts at the U- and S-Bahnhof Friedrichstrasse, in the heart of the former East Berlin, and covers the whole length of the Friedrichstrasse. The tour involves a lot of walking, but the many cafés, restaurants, shops and department stores on the way make for some pleasant shopping and eating stops.

In the 1920s, Friedrichstrasse evolved as the city's main entertainment boulevard, lined with cinemas, variety theatres and music halls. The road was widely devastated during World War II, and it seemed unlikely that it would ever regain any of its former glory. However, with the fall of the Wall, it has re-emerged as an entertainment and shopping mecca.

AROUND S-BAHNHOF FRIEDRICHSTRASSE

Start your walk at the **S-Bahnhof Friedrichstrasse ❶**, the central point of the street itself and the dividing point between its shabbier northern part and the more upmarket southern strip south of Unter den Linden. With the division of the city in 1961, the station became one of the border crossings between East and West Berlin, where visitors from the West entered and left the Socialist East.

Tränenpalast
Outside the station, a few steps north on the left-hand side of the street, is the **Tränenpalast** (Palace of Tears; Schiffbauerdamm 13; www.traenenpalast.de), a low building that functioned as the border entry and exit station (the fee for entering the GDR was 25 Deutschmarks). The station's name evokes the tragedy of separation suffered by many Berliners. After reunification in 1989, the building served as an alternative music and

culture venue (now closed) but it is now protected as a historic landmark.

NORTHERN FRIEDRICHSTRASSE

The Admiralspalast

Cross the street here and go into the large, historic building opposite, the **Admiralspalast** ❷ (Friedrichstrasse 101; tel: 030-3253 3130; www.admiralspalast.de; *see p.118*). Dating to 1910 and beautifully restored, this is one of Berlin's most historic variety theatres; the building now houses an auditorium for musical theatre, a club and the hip restaurant San Nicci and is due to open a spa in the near future. This may seem like an odd combination for a nightlife hotspot, but the Admiralspalast actually started out as a bathhouse and spa – a result of the hot spring beneath it. Fortunately, almost the entire interior of the historic spa survived World War II and will be used to refit the current building.

The Distel

Located next door, at no. 101, is one of Germany's leading political cabaret venues, the **Distel** (tel: 030-204 4704; www. distel-berlin.de), whose long tradition of policial comedy even survived the Socialist period. Note that shows are in German only, so a certain grasp of the language is obviously required in order to appreciate the majority of the jokes.

Friedrichstadtpalast

Continuing north on Friedrichstrasse, you'll cross the River Spree. Stay on the same side of the street to reach the **Friedrichstadtpalast** ❸ (Friedrichstrasse 107; tel: 030-2326 2326; www. friedrichstadtpalast.de), the largest variety theatre in Europe. The current (rather unappealing) building dates back to the Socialist period. Shows

Above from far left: close up of statues on the neoclassical Gendarmenmarkt; interior design store in the Friedrichstadt-passagen, an upmarket series of shopping malls off Friedrichstrasse.

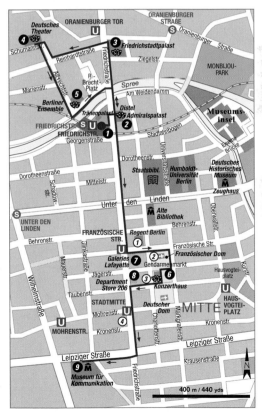

Above from left: views of the neo-classical Gendarmenmarkt; the Französischer Dom.

here contain a glamorous cocktail of showgirls in skimpy, sparkly costumes, magicians and high-flying acrobats.

German Theatres

Nearby are two rather more high-brow venues. Walk down Reinhardtstrasse and turn right onto Schumannstrasse for the **Deutsches Theater** ❹ (tel: 030-284 410; www.deutschestheater. de), generally considered to be the country's leading theatre, at no. 13a. Founded in 1850, it was made famous by that titan of the German stage, Max Reinhardt, in the early 20th century.

Just a few steps away (walk down Albrechtstrasse towards the river, then turn left on Schiffbauerdamm) is a highly regarded venue for classic modern theatre, the **Berliner Ensemble** ❺ (Bertolt-Brecht-Platz 1; tel: 030-2840 8155; www.berliner-ensemble. de), the theatre founded and managed by Bertolt Brecht. The programme primarily focuses on the plays of this 20th-century writer.

Shopping on Friedrichstrasse
Schiffbauerdamm will take you back onto Friedrichstrasse. Turn right here, and walk past the S-Bahn station once again. If you have time, follow Georgenstrasse opposite. It runs parallel to the elevated S-Bahn tracks here, and the arches under the track mostly house pubs and antiques shops.

Further south, the traffic on Friedrichstrasse becomes increasingly busy, particularly as you hit the broad, historic Unter den Linden boulevard, explored in full in tour 6 *(see p.54)*.

Continue walking southwards on Friedrichstrasse until you reach Französische Strasse, where you should turn left (east). If star-spotting appeals, take time out to visit to **Borchardt**, see ⏃①. For more star-spotting (more tricky in this case), note that just adjacent is the luxury Regent Berlin Hotel, a favourite among Hollywood stars for its seclusion.

GENDARMENMARKT

Turn right here onto Markgrafenstrasse and continue walking. You have now reached one of the city's finest squares, the magnificent, wide, open **Gendarmenmarkt** ❻, to your right. The name is derived from the French word *gendarmes* (guards), whose quarters were located here in the 1770s. The square is generally considered to be the masterpiece of the architect Karl Friedrich Schinkel (1781–1841)

Food and Drink

① BORCHARDT
Französische Strasse 47; tel: 030-8188 6262; www.borchardt-catering.de; daily 11.30am–1am; €€€
This place is one of Berlin's most renowned celebrity hangouts – a star-studded place in which to see and be seen. The food is solid, traditional French brasserie fare, with some international and Berlin dishes to appeal to local tastes, but the real attraction is the beautiful, high-ceilinged 19th-century dining room – and the clientele. In summer the best tables are in the courtyard.

for its structural harmony. It has been almost completely restored after near-total destruction during World War II.

Konzerthaus

On the Gendarmenmarkt are several buildings, including Schinkel's Ionic-porticoed **Konzerthaus** (tel: 030-203 090; www.konzerthaus.de; Mon–Sat noon–7pm, Sun noon–4pm; 75-min tours Sat 11am and 1pm; charge for tours), the former Prussian state theatre (Schauspielhaus), now a concert hall.

German and French Cathedrals

The Konzerthaus is flanked by two identical churches, the Französischer Dom (French Cathedral; tel: 030-291 760; www.franzoesischer-dom.de;

Tue–Sat noon–5pm, Sun 11am 5pm; charge) to the north, built for the immigrant Huguenots, and the Deutscher Dom (German Cathedral; tel: 030-2273 0431; www.bundestag.de; Oct–Apr: Tue– Sun 10am– 6pm, May–Sept: Tue–Sun 10am–7pm; free) to the south. Both were originally constructed in the early 18th century, with the domes added in 1785.

The Deutscher Dom now houses an exhibition on Germany's recent social and political history, cleverly combining displays of documents and photographs with radio broadcasts to chronicle the rise of Nazism and the development of democracy in Germany. The descriptive panels are all in German, but audio guides and infor-

The Huguenots

The Gendarmenmarkt is a reminder of the strong influence the Huguenots played in Berlin's culture. Emigrating from France in the 16th century, some 20,000 of these French Protestants were welcomed into Prussia. Known for their craftsmanship, their high level of education and their wealth, the Huguenots made their mark on Berlin in many ways, from additions to the local dialect to contributions to literature, science and commerce.

mation booklets are both available in English and French.

The Französischer Dom is the home of the **Hugenottenmuseum** (Huguenot Museum; tel: 030-229 1760; www.fran zoesischer-dom.de; Tue–Sat noon– 5pm, Sun 11am–5pm; charge), a museum dedicated to the Huguenots who settled in Berlin and played an instrumental part in starting the local Industrial Revolution. It is also home to **Refugium**, see ⑪②.

The church has an annex, in which there is a functioning church, the **Französische Friedrichstadtkirche**.

Treats and Refreshment

After sightseeing on the square itself, chocoholics might like to check out the nearby chocolate store **Fassbender & Rausch** (Charlottenstrasse 60; tel: 030-2045 8443; www.fassbender-rausch.de; Mon–Sun 11am–8pm), whose larger-than-life landmarks made from chocolate are worth admiring. On the same street is **Lutter & Wegner**, see ⑪③, an excellent choice for a Wiener schnitzel. Next door to Lutter & Wegner is a small wine bar that marks the spot where Sekt, the German equivalent to champagne, was first pressed.

FRIEDRICHSTADTPASSAGEN

Move away from Gendarmenmarkt now, heading past the Konzerthaus onto Taubenstrasse, which will take you all the way back to Friedrich-strasse. Stay on the same side of the street and take a look north – you will see a series of modern offices and shopping complexes stretching between Französische Strasse (to the north) to Mohrenstrasse (to the south).

These are the Friedrichstadtpassagen, a spectacular complex of shops and restaurants, with each building (called a 'quartier', the French for district) the work of a different internationally acclaimed architect. The front of the complex is on Friedrichstrasse, but there are side entrances on Mohrenstrasse, Taubenstrasse, Jägerstrasse and Französische Strasse. Note that each 'quartier' is connected to the others by underground passage.

Quartier 207

The first complex, designed by the French architect Jean Nouvel and dubbed 'Quartier 207', includes the area around Französische Strasse. Its highlight, at 76–8 Friedrichstrasse, is the only branch outside France of that country's main department store, **Galeries Lafayette** ❼ (tel: 030-209 480; www.galeries-lafayette.de; Mon–Sat 10am–8pm). This ground floor of the building features two cone-shaped glass-enclosed shapes around which the merchandise is displayed. In the basement there's an impressive gourmet foods department, where you can sample many of the products and watch cookery demonstrations.

Quartier 206

The middle complex, designed by Pei, Cobb, Freed and Partners, is an even more elegant affair. The main shop here is the upmarket fashion concept store, **Department Store 206** ❽ (Friedrichstrasse 71; 030-2094 6800; www.departmentstore-quartier206. com; Mon–Fri 11am–8pm; Sat 10am–6pm). Also within the complex are high-end boutiques, cafés and speciality stores, making this one of the most inviting areas of the Passagen.

Quartier 205

Next door (to the south) is the final part of the complex, Quartier 205, designed by O.M. Ungers. This is more low-key than its upmarket neighbours, with a larger number of budget shops and cafés. There's a good coffeeshop just opposite here, **Einstein**, see ⑪④, on Friedrichstrasse.

COMMUNICATIONS MUSEUM

Back on Friedrichstrasse, continue south, crossing the busy Leipziger Strasse. Ahead of you at this point is **Checkpoint Charlie** *(covered in tour 10, see p.74)*. Stay on Leipziger Strasse, however, until you reach no. 16, home to the **Museum für Kommunikation** ❾ (Leipziger Strasse 16; tel: 030-202 940; www.museumsstiftung.de), a museum on post and telecommunications, housed in a fine neoclassical building.

Food and Drink 🍽

② REFUGIUM

Gendarmenmarkt 5; tel: 030-229 1661; www.restaurant-refugium.de; 11am–late; €€

This upmarket French-German restaurant in the Französicher Dom is one of the best around Gendarmenmarkt, and the only one directly on the square. In summer there are also tables outside. The food mostly comprises light fish and salad dishes, with the occasional hearty Berlin game or pork offerings thrown in.

③ LUTTER & WEGNER

Charlottenstrasse 56; tel: 030-202 9540; www.lutter-wegner-gendarmenmarkt.de; daily 11am–3am; €€€

This arty, elegant Austrian-Berlin restaurant is renowned for its super-thin, crispy Wiener schnitzel served with potato salad, its delicious roasts and its rich desserts. It gets packed out nightly with a lively loyal clientele. In summer, the pavement tables are great for people-watching.

④ EINSTEIN

Friedrichstrasse 185; tel: 030-9393 6434; www.einstein-coffeeshops.com; Mon–Sat 7.30am–8.30pm, Sun 9am–8pm; €

As one of the most popular outlets of this local chain of coffee shops (there is another branch of Einstein right opposite the Galeries Lafayette), the Friedrich-strasse branch serves some of the country's best coffee and delicious sandwiches and pastry.

Above from far left: Friedrichstadt-passagen; inside Galeries Lafayette.

Above: fashions, ties and colourful gnomes – something for everyone at the Galeries Lafayette, in the Friedrich-stadtpassagen.

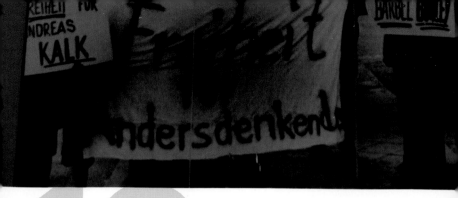

CHECKPOINT CHARLIE

On 13 August 1961 the East German Socialist regime erected a 167.8km (104-mile) long, 4.1m (13.5ft) high wall, ripping through existing districts and dividing the city into East and West. The Wall's most infamous border crossing, Checkpoint Charlie, is visited on this tour.

DISTANCE 2km (1¼ miles)
TIME Half a day
START Checkpoint Charlie
END Anhalter Bahnhof
POINTS TO NOTE
Note that Checkpoint Charlie gets particularly busy at weekends. The best way to access the area is by U-Bahn (U6 Kochstrasse) or S-Bahn (Anhalter Bahnhof station).

Above: posing at the Wall; the flags of the Allies (US, UK, France and the former USSR).

This tour starts at **Checkpoint Charlie ❶** (Friedrichstrasse 43–5; open 24 hours), at the corner of Friedrichstrasse and Kochstrasse. It gained international renown by being the only Allied border crossing for western soldiers and foreigners entering East Berlin. For Germans, the checkpoint was off-limits. For four decades, Checkpoint Charlie symbolised the clash of Western and Soviet powers more than any other location in Europe. It was here, in October 1961, for example, that Soviet and US tanks held their ground in a stand-off.

The border-crossing control station is in the middle of Friedrichstrasse. Although the one you see today is a replica, it's very similar to the real thing. Note that the Wall ran along Zimmerstrasse, just perpendicular, at this point.

Today, the area is usually packed with tourists taking pictures of the checkpoint and actors (dressed as soldiers), who pose with visitors for that Cold War shot. Adding to the atmosphere are huge portraits of western soldiers who once worked here – an art work commissioned after the western powers left Berlin in 1994.

CHECKPOINT CHARLIE MUSEUM

The history of the Wall and the courage of those who sought to escape to the West are chronicled in the **Haus am Checkpoint Charlie ❷** (House at Checkpoint Charlie; Friedrichstrasse

---

Food and Drink

① ENTRECÔTE

Schützenstrasse 5; tel: 030-2016 5496; www.entrecote.de; Mon–Fri noon–midnight, Sat 6pm–midnight, Sun 6pm–11pm; €€
Cosy Entrecôte is popular for its skinny French fries, great steaks with sauce Béarnaise and friendly, understated service.

43–5; tel: 030-253 7250; www.mauer museum.de; daily 9am–10pm; charge). Although rather touristy, it does a good job of documenting the ingenious attempts made by East Germans to crack the Wall, using methods from high-flying balloons to specially prepared cars, tunnels and more. The museum also tells of the estimated 125 to 206 victims (the correct number is still debated) who were shot by the East German border patrols.

PETER FECHTER MEMORIAL

One of the most famous of these victims was 18-year-old Peter Fechter, who almost made it to the West on 17 August 1962, but was shot by a patrol guard and left bleeding to death for hours in the no man's land between East and West. To the protests of a West Berlin crowd, neither the Allied soldiers nor West Berlin's police interfered, as this would have been a violation of East German territory. The East German border guards finally removed his body.

The spot on which he was killed is now marked by a small memorial, the **Peter Fechter Memorial ❸**. To reach it, turn right on Friedrichstrasse as you leave the museum, then take a right into Zimmerstrasse. Walk for a few metres, and you'll see the memorial on the left-hand side of the street, between Charlotten- and Markgrafenstrasse.

If you are hungry at this point, **Entrecôte**, see ⑪①, is just nearby.

Above from far left: exhibits showing freedom-fighters and their 'Freedom for those who think Differently' banners; the grim, grey Wall.

What's in a Name?
Checkpoint Charlie was established in August 1961 as one of three American-controlled border points in Berlin and on the East–West German border. Each of these was given a letter from the air-traffic control alphabet: 'Alpha' was the checkpoint in Helmstedt (the start of one of the autobahn corridors leading through the East to Berlin); 'Bravo' was the checkpoint in Berlin-Dreilinden (the end of that same corridor); 'Charlie' was the inner-city checkpoint.

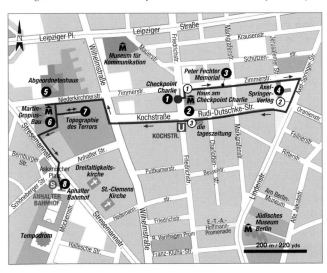

Above from left:
the Wall at the
Topographie
des Terrors; visitors
taking in the site's
full horror.

Axel Springer
Axel-Springer-Verlag's
founder, Axel Cäsar
Springer, was one
of the world's most
illustrious publishing
figureheads and an
adamant campaigner
for German re-
unification. It was for
this reason that he
built his headquarters
close to the Wall.
From here, his
newspapers, notably
the tabloid *Bild*,
not only evolved
as one of the most
aggressive critics of
Socialism, but also
became the target for
the 1960s militant
student movement.

AXEL-SPRINGER-VERLAG

Now continue walking down Zimmer-strasse, and imagine that you would have been walking in the shadow of the Wall to your left. At the end of Zimmerstrasse, you'll hit Axel-Springer-Strasse. Turn right, then right again onto Rudi-Dutschke-Strasse. The high-rise building before you houses the headquarters of the **Axel-Springer-Verlag** ❹ (Markgrafenstrasse 19a; tel: 030-25910; www.axel-springer-passage. de; opening hours differ from shop to shop), one of Europe's largest publishing houses *(see margin left)* and the Axel-Springer-Passagen shopping mall. A good pitstop here, if you need one, is **Mittelbar**, see ⑪②.

Things were not always so peaceful here. In 1967–8, the area saw brutal clashes between the police and students protesting against Capitalism and the Vietnam War. *Bild* delivery trucks went up in flames, and windows were shattered. Germany's student leader Rudi Dutschke became the national figurehead of left-wing politics, also leading the protest against the conservative Springer company.

RUDI-DUTSCHKE-STRASSE

Irony has it that the street on which you are now standing, right in front of the Axel-Springer building, is called Rudi-Dutschke-Strasse, despite the protests of the publishing company

and conservatives. However, after a popular vote in the district, this section of Kochstrasse was renamed in 2008 – a somewhat belated victory for the 1968 student movement.

KOCHSTRASSE

Walking down Kochstrasse takes you into an area that was its journalistic headquarters in the 1920s. Today – apart from the Springer-Verlag – only a few papers are still based in this area, including, in a 19th-century building to your left, Germany's largest left-wing newspaper, the *Tageszeitung*.

If you want to rub shoulders with the media (and perhaps some politicians too), grab a chair at the Italian **Sale e Tabacchi**, see ⑪③, just next door.

NIEDERKIRCHNERSTRASSE

Further down Kochstrasse, you will pass Checkpoint Charlie again. After crossing Wilhelmstrasse, walk north to the cobbled Niederkirchnerstrasse, which you should then follow. To the left, you should be able to see one of the few remaining, original sections of the Wall. Note the many holes revealing the iron grid in the concrete; these are the work of so-called 'Mauer-spechte' (literally 'wall woodpeckers') – East and West Berliners, who, in the first days after the fall of the Wall, simply took their hammers out to carve out their own mementoes.

Abgeordnetenhaus and Martin-Gropius-Bau

Sights on Niederkirchnerstrasse include the **Abgeordnetenhaus ⑤** (Niederkirchnerstrasse 5; tel: 030-2325 1064; Sun–Wed 9am–6pm, Thur–Sat 9am–10pm), the State Assembly of Berlin, which you can peek inside. On the same street is the impressive **Martin-Gropius-Bau ⑥** (Niederkirchnerstrasse 7; tel: 030-254 860; www.gropiusbau.de; Wed–Mon 10am–8pm). Originally built as an Arts and Crafts museum in 1877–81, the building is now fully restored and showcases large-scale artistic and historical exhibits, as well as (on the upper floors) photography collections.

Topography of Terror

As is often the case in Berlin, grand and gruesome history are never far from each other. When leaving the museum, turn back around towards the adjacent wide open area (the space behind the part of the Wall you've just passed). The cellars, which are presented as open pits, are part of the **Topographie des Terrors ⑦** (Niederkirchnerstrasse 8; tel: 030-2545 0950; www.topographie.de; Oct–Apr: daily 10am–6pm, May–Sept: daily 10am–8pm; free), showcasing the original, now excavated torture cellars of the SS, Hitler's most loyal and brutal security force, which had its Berlin headquarters here.

In the first months after Hitler's rise to power, opponents of the regime were brought here, into 'wild' prisons, which were still in use until the end of the war. A small exhibition explains the history of the area; a documentary centre is planned for the future.

ANHALTER BAHNHOF

Now come out onto Stresemannstrasse and turn left. After a few steps, you will cross Askanischer Platz, behind which is the restored entrance portico to the **Anhalter Bahnhof ⑧** (Askanischer Platz 6), once Berlin's largest railway station. Built in 1876–80 by the industrial architect Franz Schwechten, it was damaged in World War II and later demolished. Today all that remains is this portico. By an irony of latter-day history, Schwechten was also the architect of the Kaiser-Wilhelm-Gedächtniskirche *(see p.33)*, another of the city's noble ruins.

Exile from Berlin

The westbound platform of the Anhalter Bahnhof staged the tragic last act of the Weimar Republic: soon after Hitler became Chancellor, Berlin's most gifted artists and intellectuals – among them Heinrich Mann, Bertolt Brecht, Kurt Weill, Georg Grosz and Albert Einstein – gathered here, their bags packed for the 'last train to freedom'. The station was patched up after the war, but after the border was sealed it stood at the end of a line to nowhere, and became redundant.

Food and Drink 🍴

② MITTELBAR IM AXEL-SPRINGER-PASSAGE
Markgrafenstrasse 19a; tel: 030-2591 74850; www.mittelbar.de; Mon–Fri 9am–7pm; €
The Mittelbar is a relaxed bistro in the Axel-Springer-Passagen. Popular among journalists working here, it serves a limited but tasty international menu from Club sandwiches to Yakitori. Good cocktails, coffees and teas.

③ SALE E TABACCHI
Rudi-Dutschke-Strasse 23; tel: 030-252 1155; www.sale-e-tabacchi.de; daily 10am–late; €€
This no-nonsense Italian restaurant welcomes a media and political crowd, who like to argue over delicious pasta or seafood dishes. In summer, the courtyard is very inviting. Great-value set menus at lunch.

KREUZBERG

Kreuzberg has had a tumultuous history. Once a working-class industrial quarter, it was heavily bombed in World War II. In the shadow of the Wall, it was brought back to life by Turkish immigrants, hippies and radicals. Today, artists, clubbers and the Turkish–German community maintain its vibrancy.

DISTANCE 10.5km (6½ miles)
TIME A full day
START Hallesches Tor
END Schlesisches Tor
POINTS TO NOTE
If your feet get tired during this long walk, you may wish to skip some sections and take the U-Bahn instead. At several points in the route, you will find stations on U-Bahn line 1 just a short distance away.

SO 36 Club
Kreuzberg has been a focus for many key development's in the city's music scene. The SO 36 Club (at Oranienstrasse 190; www.so36.de) was historically home to Berlin's punk rock movement, and in the 1970s was often frequented by David Bowie (shown above in an exhibit at the Schwules Museum) and Iggy Pop.

Above from left: café on bohemian Bergmannstrasse; chillis at the Turkish Market; the Schwules Museum; arty Bergmannstrasse.

Food and Drink 🍴
① OSTERIA NUMERO UNO
Kreuzbergstrasse 71; 030-786 9162; www.osteria-uno.de; daily noon–1am; €€
This welcoming trattoria is probably the best choice among Kreuzberg's Italian restaurants. Its ultra-thin, crispy pizzas ensure a loyal crowd of regular customers. Antipasti, salads and pasta are also on the menu. At weekends, locals flock here for breakfast or lunch and then spend a lazy afternoon in Viktoria-park behind the restaurant.

When the Wall went up, Kreuzberg (the name means 'Cross Hill') became an isolated pocket of West Berlin. Many buildings were abandoned and the cheap rents enticed Turkish guest-workers, while empty houses attracted squatters. Before long, it was one of Berlin's most vibrant areas, both culturally and politically. Since the Wall came down, however, it has become a more fashionable place to live, and rents have gone up considerably. Yet despite the pressures of gentrification, the area retains an air of radicalism and has become a centre for the arts scene, with a buzzing nightlife to match.

Kreuzberg's historic postcodes are still used by locals to refer to the district's distinct areas. The edgier part to the east is known as 'SO 36' after its pre-war postcode. This chunk of neighbourhood is packed with Turkish shops, cafés and alternative bookshops and is also the location of Böcklerpark and Görlitzer Park. In the southwest of Kreuzberg is the more middle-class 'SW 61'. In this section's southwestern corner is Vik-toriapark, while in the most directly southern part is the Nazi-era airport, Flughafen Tempelhof (now closed).

HALLESCHES TOR

The **Hallesches Tor ❶** is one of the area's seven U-Bahn stations elevated above street level on iron piers. Leave the station on the Tempelhofer Ufer side, and then take a left turn to walk south on Mehringdamm, one of Kreuzberg's major thoroughfares.

GAY MUSEUM

Follow the bustling street life south and find the **Schwules Museum ❷** (Mehringdamm 61; tel: 030-6959 9050, www.schwulesmuseum.de; Sun–Mon and Wed–Fri 2–6pm, Sat 2–7pm; charge). For years, this was the world's only museum devoted to gay

life and culture. Its library contains archives of noted sexologists as well as thousands of books and periodicals. Plenty of information is available in English at the museum.

VIKTORIAPARK

When you've finished there, turn right off Mehringdamm onto Kreuzberg-strasse, and, if you are ready for a break, pop into **Osteria Numero Uno**, see ⓐ①. Afterwards, head west on Kreuzbergstrasse to visit **Viktoriapark ❸** (daily; free). Originally laid out in the 19th century for hard-working local residents, it comprises winding trails, rocky areas and a deep water-fall. Follow the paths up to the 66m

Jewish Museum
Slightly northeast of Hallesches Tor is the Jüdisches Museum (Lindenstrasse 9–14; tel: 030-2599 3300; www.juedisches-museum-berlin.de; Tue–Sun 10am–8pm, Mon 10am–10pm; charge). Designed by Daniel Libeskind, it concentrates on Jewish life in Germany through art, artefacts, documents and films. Jewish contributions to German culture are made plain, and Germany's anti-Semitism is addressed without blinking, as is the Holocaust.

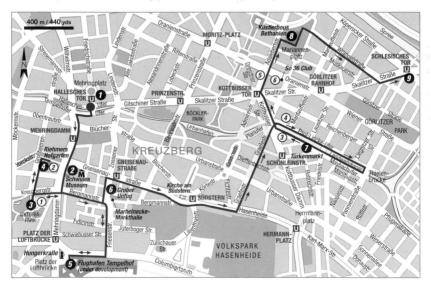

(217ft) high Kreuzberg, the hill after which the district is named. At the top is a 19th-century Prussian memorial designed by the architect Karl Friedrich Schinkel to commemorate the wars against Napoleon. From here, there are great views across the city.

RIEHMERS HOFGARTEN

When you have finished in the park, return to Kreuzbergstrasse and then follow Grossbeerenstrasse north, before turning right onto Yorckstrasse. On your right after a few metres/yards you should see the beautifully restored tenement-house complex of the **Riehmers Hofgarten** ❹ (Yorckstrasse 83–6). Built in 1891–2 for young army officers, the building epitomises the restrained neoclassical style of Imperial Germany. Today, the complex – with its quiet, interconnected courtyards – accommodates a hotel *(see p.113)* as well as the **E.T.A. Hoffmann** restaurant, see ⑪②.

BERGMANNSTRASSE

At this point on the tour, retrace your steps back to Kreuzbergstrasse and head east, continuing over the crossroads to Bergmannstrasse. This is one of the most lively and interesting parts of Kreuzberg, with a proliferation of quirky, independent shops, cafés, pubs and restaurants. This area is absolutely typical of what Berliners refer to as a 'Kiez', meaning a tightly knit neighbourhood community.

TEMPELHOF AIRPORT

The streets running south off Bergmannstrasse (such as Friesenstrasse) lead to the old Nazi-era airport, **Flughafen Tempelhof** ❺ (Platz der Luftbrücke 5). Built in 1936–9 by Ernst Sagebiel in a Fascist style, it is laid out on an epic scale, and, in its time, was one of the world's most technically advanced airports. After World War II, it became famous as the setting for the Berlin Airlift in 1948–9, after the Soviets cut off overland routes into West Berlin. For 11 months, British and American planes – landing just as others were taking off from the same runway – kept all of the Allied sectors supplied. The 'Hungerkralle' monument, a fork-like stone monument, in front of the terminal, is a reminder of the heroism of the pilots. The airport finally closed in 2008 and is currently used as a venue for fashion shows and music festivals.

AROUND GNEISENAUSTRASSE

Returning to Bergmannstrasse via Friesenstrasse, keep walking north on Zossener Strasse, passing the comic store and Kreuzberg landmark, the **Grober Unfug** ❻ (Zossener Strasse 33; tel: 030-6940 1490; www.grober

unfug.de; Mon–Fri 11am–7pm, Sat 11am–6pm). When you hit Gneisenaustrasse, turn right, heading east. Keep going for several minutes, walking straight past the Kirche am Südstern (a church) onto Hasenheide. On this street, look out for the turning for Graefestrasse on your left and head north into a neighbourhood full of nicely restored tenements – the Graefekiez. Eventually, Graefestrasse leads to the Kottbusser Tor (Kottbusser Gate, *see p.82*), on the Landwehrkanal in the heart of 'SW 61'.

Cross the bridge and, if you are in need of a pitstop after all the walking, drop by the **Ankerklause**, see ⑪③, a small bar and café on the canal. On the far side of the canal, turn right (east) and walk down Paul-Lincke-Ufer. This more affluent area contains some of the district's finest late 19th-century mansions. It is a pleasant place for a stroll, and there are many cafés and restaurants where you can linger for longer if you so wish. One of the best of these is **Café am Ufer**, see ⑪④.

Turkish Market

After following the canal all the way to the Thielenbrücke (Thielen Bridge), cross over to the other side again and

Above: textiles and fresh vegetables at the Turkish Market.

Market Hall
Only a handful of Berlin's 19th-century market halls remain in operation. One of the liveliest is the Marheinecke-Markthalle (Beusselstrasse 44 N-Q; tel: 030-398 9610; www.meine-markthalle.de; Mon–Fri 8am–8pm, Sat 8am–6pm, Sun closed; free), located just to the south of Gneisenaustrasse. The market specialises in offering fresh produce from across Europe.

Food and Drink 🍴

② E.T.A. HOFMANN
Yorckstrasse 83; tel: 030-7809 8809; www.restaurant-e-t-a-hoffmann.de; Wed–Mon 5pm–late; €€€
Located within the Riehmers Hofgarten Hotel *(see p.113)*, this upmarket restaurant specialises in modern German cuisine prepared by Thomas Kurt, one of Berlin's finest chefs. Considering the quality of the food, the prices are remarkably restrained.

③ ANKERKLAUSE
Kottbusser Damm 104; tel: 030-693 5649; www.ankerklause.de; daily 10am–late; €
One of Kreuzberg's liveliest late-night watering holes, the Ankerklause is popular with students and a young trendy crowd. In summer, the party spills out onto the banks of the Landwehrkanal.

④ CAFÉ AM UFER
Paul-Lincke-Ufer 42; tel: 030-6162 9200; www.cafe-am-ufer.de; daily 10am–late; €€
This friendly café is renowned locally for its sumptuous breakfasts. At other times of day, it also serves tasty French and German dishes. In summer there is seating in the front garden, with a pleasant outlook onto the neighbourhood and the Landwehrkanal.

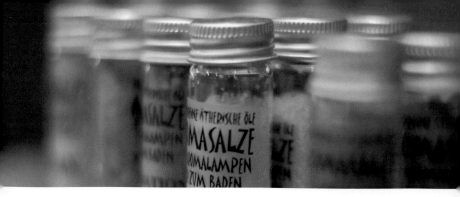

Above: in Kreuzberg, funky lifestyle stores such as Belladonna (above) and fashion boutiques including Irie Daily (opposite), sit side by side with traditional Turkish grocery stores.

follow it back to the **Türkenmarkt ❼** (Maybachufer; tel: 030-781 5844; Tue and Fri noon–6.30pm; free), where, twice a week, fresh vegetables, spices and a huge number of different varieties of olives can be purchased.

When you have reached the western end of the canal again, turn right onto Kottbusser Damm and head northwards. Soon, you will reach a large roundabout where there is a major U-Bahn station, **Kottbusser Tor** (Kottbusser Gate).

On the far side, before continuing on to Adalebertstrasse, you may wish to take a detour off to the left on Dresdner Strasse to find **Hasir**, see ⑪⑤. This is one of the oldest Turkish restaurants in Berlin. It may look a little dingy from the outside, but the food inside is excellent.

ORANIENSTRASSE

Back on Adalebertstrasse, within a few metres/yards you will reach Oranienstrasse, crossing east–west. This is SO 36's unofficial high street, is lined with urban fashion boutiques, traditional Turkish grocery stores, cafés and alternative bookshops.

During the 1960s and 1970s, this area was at the heart of Berlin's student movement. At that time, the tenements had not yet been renovated, rents were extremely low, and new social arrangements from 'Wohngemeinschaft' (flat-shares) to 'free love' were being tried out.

A hint of the atmosphere of those days can still be felt in the old-style pub, the **Rote Harfe**, see ⑪⑥, located just off Oranienplatz.

Gay and Arty Schöneberg

The neighbouring district of Schöneberg is a bohemian enclave as noted for its gay scene as for its artistic culture. With a population of some 300,000, and governed by a gay mayor, Berlin's gay community is open and relaxed. By the 1920s, the area around Motzstrasse was already a gay centre, thanks in part to the Eldorado Club (where Christopher Isherwood, author of *Berlin Stories*, was a regular). When the Nazis came to power, however, homosexual people were forced to wear a pink triangle on their clothing and many were sent to concentration camps. Estimates of the number that perished range from 5,000 to 15,000. Today, a monument to them is affixed to the Nollendorfplatz U-Bahn station near Motzstrasse. After the war, the West German government held homosexuality in legal limbo, though the East German regime decriminalised it in the early 1950s. Nowadays, the scene is still very much where it used to be: in the Motzkiez (Motzstrasse, Oranienstrasse and Mehringdamm) in the West and in Prenzlauer Berg (Gleimstrasse and Greifenhagener Strasse) in the East.

MARIANNENPLATZ

Radical traditions are also kept up with the annual May Day parties, centring on Mariannenplatz to the north of Oranienstrasse via Adalebertstrasse.

In years past, May Day was riot day in East Kreuzberg. Supermarkets were ritually trashed and confrontations with the police were *de rigueur*. Nowadays the event is a little tamer, and 24 hours of political demonstrations have been replaced with a less aggressive day of hedonism. All the same, the walls of buildings around these parts are still covered with graffiti and political posters all year round and form a good barometer of the hot issues of the day.

Bethanien Art Centre

Also located at Mariannenplatz – though a somewhat calmer enterprise – is the **Künstlerhaus Bethanien** ❽ (Bethanien Art Centre; Mariannenplatz 2; tel: 030-616 9030; www.bethanien.de; Wed–Sun 2–7pm; free). This publicly sponsored art centre occupies a former hospital complex, and retains an almost cloistral atmosphere. There are usually exhibitions by the artists who work here, and, on some days, studios are open to the public.

SCHLESISCHES TOR

Now leave Mariannenplatz and take Wrangelstrasse off to the east. When you finally meet Skalitzer Strasse, turn left and follow the road up to the **Schlesisches Tor** ❾ (Schlesisches Gate), where this tour ends. When Berlin was still divided by the Wall, this was also the last U-Bahn stop in West Berlin before meeting the River Spree; East Berlin was just on the other side.

While in times past this neighbourhood had a slightly sinister feel to it, today it bears all the signs of regeneration, as the fine old warehouses on the river banks are redeveloped for media and high-tech companies. If you so wish, you can get a feeling for this transition by exploring to the south on Schlesische Strasse.

Old Industries
Before World War II, Ritterstrasse (to the south of Oranienstrasse) was known as the 'Export Quarter', while Kochstrasse (to the west of Oranienstrasse) was the 'Press Quarter'. The latter was home to many of the country's largest newspapers, as well as several publishers. Both these quarters were almost completely destroyed during an Allied bombing raid on 3 February 1945.

Food and Drink 🍴

⑤ HASIR
Adalebertstrasse 10; tel: 030-614 2373; www.hasir.de; 9am–5am; €
The first in this small chain of inexpensive Turkish 'Imbisse' is still the best. Mouth-watering lamb and chicken dishes attract a mixed clientele of Turkish locals in the evenings and young people out on the town during the night.

⑥ ROTE HARFE
Oranienstrasse 13/Heinrichplatz; tel: 030-618 4446; www.roteharfe.de; Mon–Sat 10am–late, Sun 9am–late; €
This old-style student pub takes you back to the 1960s and 1970s. The 'Red Harp' offers simple but hearty food, good music and a great atmosphere.

PRENZLAUER BERG

This once working-class district remained largely unscathed during the war, and its large number of undamaged buildings attracted the first redevelopers after the fall of the Wall. Today, Prenzlauer Berg is upscale – popular with a 20- and 30-something crowd, particularly fashionable young families.

DISTANCE 2km (1¼ miles)
TIME Half a day
START Senefelder Platz
END Kulturbrauerei
POINTS TO NOTE
This tour leads through one of the city's most attractive districts. At weekends, note that the main hubs (around Kollwitzplatz) can get quite crowded. To reach the starting point, take the U-Bahn to the stop of the same name. Note that if you want to visit the synagogue, its opening times are very limited *(see p.87)*.

Berlin is so flat that the gentle rise on which this neighbourhood sits earned it the half-ironic status of a 'mountain'. Until the last half of the 19th century, that rise was sufficient to catch the prevailing winds, and so Prenzlauer Berg was Berlin's milling centre, with dozens of windmills providing flour to the city's bakeries. Then came the breweries, with Joseph Pfeffer opening the first in 1841 at the site on Schönhauser Allee, which is now the entertainment complex Pfefferberg. In 1853, Jost Schultheiss took over a brewery at Schönhauser Allee and built his empire there; today, it is the Kulturbrauerei *(see p.87)*. Others followed, such as the Bötzow on Prenzlauer Allee and Königstadt on Saarbrücker Strasse.

The district's real expansion came towards the end of the century, when workers' housing, so-called 'Mietskasernen' (rental-barracks), was thrown up in a frenzy of construction to house the thousands of new Berliners attracted by the industry that had grown up in the city.

20th Century and Beyond

With little industry and much housing, the district was spared the bombing of World War II, and although the GDR did little to rebuild or renovate the Mietskasernen, they still survived. The spacious apartments attracted East German intellectuals and artists, particularly around Kollwitzplatz *(see p.86)* and local cafés such as the Westphal (now the Istoria restaurant) at Kollwitzstrasse 64 was a meeting place for dissident intellectuals. Another centre of dissent was the Gesemanekirche (Gol-

gotha Church) on Stargarder Strasse *(see p.86)*, some of whose parishioners had been involved in the sheltering of Jews during the Nazi regime.

After the Wall came down, the cheap apartments drew a new group of bohemians. The so-called LSD district (named after the boundary streets, Lychener Strasse, Stargarder Strasse and Danziger Strasse) became a hotbed for creativity. The area south of Danziger Strasse, between Schönhauser Allee and Prenzlauer Allee, became notably chic. Today, Prenzlauer Berg's bars and restaurants attract a multilingual crowd of young late 20- and 30-something professionals.

SENEFELDER PLATZ

This tour starts on **Senefelder Platz ❶**, named after the inventor of lithography, Alois Senefelder (1771–1834). The architecture you see here – of five- to six-storey tenement houses – is highly typical of the district: some 120 years ago, these houses were crammed with working-class families, often occupying a single room, with no flowing water and with communal bathrooms.

Public bathrooms were typical at this time, and one of the finest examples of these – 'Café Achteck' (Octagonal Café) as Berliners call them – can be found on the square. The dark-green, wrought-iron block houses fully functioning urinals, although there are no facilities for women.

JEWISH CEMETERY

From here, walk north on Schönhauser Allee, the wide boulevard that runs through the district. After a few steps, you will pass the **Jüdischer Friedhof ❷** (Jewish Cemetery; Schönhauser Allee 23), founded in 1827. This is the last resting place of several prominent Jewish-German figures including the composer Giacomo Meyerbeer, the 20th-century painter Max Liebermann and the publisher Leopold Ullstein, as well as many well-to-do merchants, intellectuals and families from the 19th and early 20th centuries. Take a leisurely stroll through the cemetery if time allows.

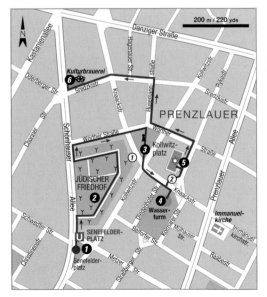

Prenzlauer Berg Churches

The churches in Prenzlauer Berg played a significant role in the years during and after World War II, some as safe havens, some as meeting places for dissidents. Key churches include the Gothic-Revival Gethsemanekirche, at Stargarder Strasse 77 (very limited opening hours, tel: 030-445 7745 for details) and the Zionskirche (Zionskirchplatz; tel: 030-8870 9870; www.zionskirche-berlin.de; Mon 8–10pm, Thur 10am–8pm, Sun noon–4pm; free). The latter, a Protestant church, built between 1866 and 1873, served as a resistance cell during the Nazi period. It is also famous for its 'Umweltbibliothek' (Environmental Library), an unofficial political information centre founded in the 1980s and a considerable force in East Berlin, where freedom of speech was banned.

Right: arty building in Prenzlauer Berg.

KOLLWITZPLATZ

Come out of the cemetery and get back onto Schönhauser Allee, heading north. Turn right onto Wörther Strasse to reach the area's main square, **Kollwitzplatz ❸**, named after Käthe Kollwitz (1867–1945), one of Germany's most prominent female painters and sculptors. Renowned for her strong social conscience, she depicted such subjects as the horrors of war and the harsh realities of working-class life. She lived on Kollwitzstrasse until the 1940s, although the building concerned is no longer standing. Note her sculpture *Motherly Love* on the square.

The main action on and around Kollwitzplatz, particularly in the surrounding streets such as Wörtherstrasse, Knaackstrasse and Kollwitzstrasse, is admittedly, rather less worthy. This is one of Berlin's most popular nightspots, known for its proliferation of bars, 'Kneipen' (pubs), cafés and restaurants. An excellent way to soak in the atmosphere (particularly in the evenings) is to take time out in the French-German restaurant **Gugelhof**, see ⑪①, on the square.

WATER TOWER

Walk across the square and follow Knaackstrasse to the **Wasserturm ❹** (Knaackstrasse 23). Standing on a little

hill, this 1877 water tower is now out of use, but is still Prenzlauer Berg's unofficial landmark. During Nazi times, it was a secret detention centre for political prisoners.

There are even more pubs, cafés and restaurants at this point, among them **Pasternak**, see ⑪②.

SYNAGOGUE

From Knaackstrasse, turn left (north) into narrow Rykestrasse for the **Synagogue** ❺ (Rykestrasse 53; tel: 030-8802 8316; www.synagoge-rykestrasse. de; Thur 2–5pm, Sun 1–5pm; charge, incl. guided tour), one of the few historic synagogues that survived the brutality of the Nazi progroms in November 1938. This building miraculously survived intact owing to its position wedged between tenement houses – if it had been set fire to, the adjacent homes would have also burned down. The synagogue's opening times are limited, but if you are here on Thursday or Sunday afternoons, it's worth a visit for the insight it gives into the life of the once-thriving Jewish community in this area.

HUSEMANNSTRASSE

From the synagogue, continue heading north on Rykestrasse, then turn left onto Wörtherstrasse. From here, turn right into Husemannstrasse. This street – one of the best-preserved in the city with its magnificent 19th-century houses – is gorgeous, particularly in summer, when the large trees here afford welcome shade. It is peppered with antiques shops and cafés.

KULTURBRAUEREI

After browsing Husemannstrasse, turn left onto Sredzkistrasse, then take another right back onto Schönhauser Alle, for the entrance to the **Kulturbrauerei** ❻ (Schönhauser Allee 36; tel: 030-443 5260; www.kulturbrauerei-berlin.de). Home to the former Schultheiss Brewery (one of Berlin's most famous brands of beer), it is now an arts and entertainment complex, housing a cinema, theatres, shops and pubs. Take a break here to end the tour.

Food and Drink 🍴

① GUGELHOF
Kollwitzplatz/Knaackstrasse 37; tel: 030-442 9229; www.gugelhof.de; Mon–Fri 4pm–1am, Sat–Sun 10am–1am; €€
Gugelhof does hearty French, Alsatian, Swiss and German fare, served by very friendly staff in a cosy dining room, complete with creaking wooden floors and well-worn furniture. It gained notoriety when former US President Bill Clinton dined here.

② PASTERNAK
Knaackstrasse 22–4; tel: 030-441 3399; www.restaurant-pasternak.de; Mon–Sun 9am–1am; €
This cosy Russian eatery is a popular hangout for students, artists and, not surprisingly, Russians as well as Eastern Europeans. The menu includes traditional Russian fare, as well as Jewish favourites and some international dishes. The two-course lunch menus are dirt cheap.

FRIEDRICHSHAIN

Friedrichshain has changed since the Wall came down from run-down-edgy to trendy-edgy, popular with a young artistic, party crowd. The key sight is the East Side Gallery, the longest stretch of the Wall still intact, painted by artists.

DISTANCE 4.5km (3 miles)
TIME Half a day
START Alexanderplatz
END East Side Gallery
POINTS TO NOTE
To reach the Karl-Marx-Allee by public transport, catch trains either to Alexanderplatz (S- and U-Bahn) or (to cut down on the walking distance) Frankfurter Tor (U-Bahn.

Above: in their day, the Socialist-era high-rise apartments lining the Karl-Marx Allee were extremely stylish; nowadays, their appeal is rather more retro.

In recent years, Friedrichshain has become a big favourite with Berlin's younger crowd; some consider it the city's most happening district. Parts of the area are still quite rough around the edges, with cheap rents and an edgy crowd. In other parts the developers have moved in – over the river from the East Side Gallery *(see p.89)*, for example, is a huge new entertainment complex.

Food and Drink

① FLOATING LOUNGE

Mühlenstrasse 73–7; tel: 030-6676 3806; www.eastern-comfort.de; Tue–Sat 2pm–late, Sun 11am–late; €
Next to the East Side Gallery is the Eastern Comfort Hostel Boat *(see p.113)*, a houseboat-cum-hotel. Its chilled-out lounge is a quirky choice for drinks in hip Friedrichshain.

KARL-MARX-ALLEE

Start your walk at the **Alexanderplatz** ❶ and walk east onto **Karl-Marx-Allee**, an east–west route stretching 2.5km (1²⁄₃ miles). It is worth coming here to look at the façades of the Stalin-esque-style apartment blocks that line the avenue on both sides, and which, as far as the **Frankfurter Tor** ❷, have been superbly restored. Karl-Marx-Allee was laid out in the 1950s – its construction envisioned not only to create jobs in post-World War II East Berlin but also to reflect the Socialist regime's prowess in turning East Berlin into a showcase for modern architecture.

TOWARDS THE RIVER

From the Karl-Marx-Allee, take the Strasse der Pariser Kommune south, in the direction of the river, and explore the side streets here, such as Boxhagener Strasse and its adjacent square. This part of Friedrichshain is where things really get going in the evenings.

East Side Gallery

South of Karl-Marx-Allee along Mühlenstrasse, between Ostbahnhof and the

fairytale-like Oberbaumbrücke (1896), a 1.2km (³⁄₄-mile) section of the Berlin Wall has been preserved as the **East Side Gallery** ❸. A variety of international artists painted murals here in 1990, after the collapse of the Wall, and some of these works have since been restored. You can still see a number of the iconic images of that era, including *Brotherly Kiss* by Dimitri Vrubel, depicting Leonid Brezhnev and Erich Honecker in fond embrace.

On the late afternoons in summer, the river banks behind the East Side Gallery are turned into a kind of beach/bar area (Strandbar Mitte is the most attractive part). If you fancy a drink near here, pop into the funky **Floating Lounge**, see ⑪①.

O2 Arena

On the other side of Mühlenstrasse, you can't miss the vast spaceship-like **O2 World Arena** ❹ (Mühlenstrasse 12–30; tel: 01803-206 070; www.o2 world.de; *see p.121*), which hosts pop concerts, sporting events, etc. Its arrival in 2008 underlined the changes in the area, long of appeal only to an edgier crowd. These days, the banks of the Spree in Friedrichshain and in the adjacent Kreuzberg are undergoing urban regeneration, attracting businesses and, in new apartments, residents alike.

Above: the East Side Gallery.

Stasi Sights

To many East Germans, this area symbolises political oppression, with the secret service police headquarters and jails being located to the north of the area covered in this tour. The first is the Stasi Museum (Ruschestrasse 103, Haus 1; tel: 030-553 6854; www.stasimuseum.de; Mon–Fri 11am–6pm, Sat, Sun 2–6pm; charge), a research centre and museum located in the former Stasi headquarters. Further north still, at the Stiftung Gedenkstätte Berlin-Hohenschönhausen (Berlin Hohenschönhausen Memorial; Genslerstrasse 66; tel: 030-9860 8230; www.stiftung-hsh.de; charge), is one of the oldest and most brutal Stasi prisons, used for holding and interrogating presumed political opponents of the regime. You can go on a guided tour of the site, with some tours led by former inmates.

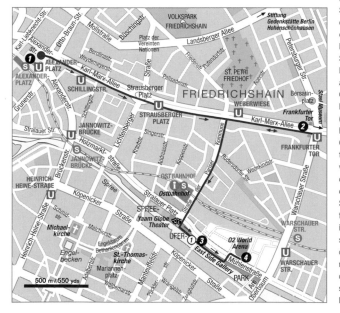

POTSDAM

Potsdam started out as a rough garrison city and only later evolved into the site of the main royal Prussian residence. It is now the capital of the state of Brandenburg. Most visitors come for the Sanssouci Palace and its gardens.

Above: park statues.

DISTANCE 10km (6¼ miles)

TIME A full day

START/END Potsdam-Hauptbahnhof (S-Bahn and mainline)

POINTS TO NOTE

To reach the starting point from central Berlin by train, take line 7 on the S-Bahn, which runs every 10 minutes to Potsdam Hauptbahnhof (about 35 mins), or a regional train from Berlin Hauptbahnhof or Bahnhof Zoo to Potsdam Hauptbahnhof (journey takes about 20 mins, but trains leave less frequently) . For the purpose of fares, Potsdam is in zone C *(see p.107)*. For a more picturesque arrival, get off the S-Bahn at Wannsee and continue by boat, or take bus 316 to Glienicker Brücke and continue by tram 93 to Potsdam town centre. Note that Sanssouci gets very busy at weekends, and that most palaces can only be visited on guided tours (separate charges for each), which can be booked at the main palace. The timing can be limiting, especially outside of the main May to October season.

Situated 30km (19 miles) southwest of Berlin, Potsdam is a small city of considerable historical importance. Its main attraction is Sanssouci Palace, built for Frederick the Great (1712–86). The entire park is a Unesco World Heritage site and contains numerous buildings, large and small, which can take a whole day to explore. Potsdam itself has an attractive city centre, studded with 18th-century buildings, including entire neighbourhoods built to look entirely Dutch and Russian.

POTSDAM TOWN

From **Potsdam Hauptbahnhof ❶** you can either catch a bus (no. 695 or X15) from outside the station to Sanssouci, or you can walk (it's about 2.5km/1½ miles). If you decide to walk, go north from the train station across to the **Alter Markt ❷**, with its 1830 neoclassical **Nikolaikirche** (Am Alten Markt; tel: 0331-270 8602; www.nikolaipotsdam.de; daily 9am–5pm, free), designed by Karl Friedrich Schinkel. Its dome bears a striking resemblance to that of St Paul's Cathedral in London.

Opposite, on the other side of the Havel, is the Baroque Town Hall, com-

Above from far left:
Schloss Sansoucci;
35 enormous caryatids
support the roof.

pleted in 1753. The Old Town, which is full of fine Baroque townhouses, has three historic gates, the Brandenburger Tor (*see below*), the Jägertor (1773) and the Nauener Tor (1755). Beyond the last (just to the north) lies the attractive **Holländisches Viertel** (Dutch quarter), built between 1734 and 1741 by Jan Boumann for Dutch settlers.

Turn left into Brandenburger Strasse, unless you need refreshment, in which case take a little detour two streets north, for **Juliette**, see ⑨①.

At the end of Brandenburger Strasse, you'll reach the imposing **Brandenburger Tor ❸**, built in 1770. Turn right here, into Schopenhauerstrasse, which leads to Sanssouci.

SANSSOUCI

Potsdam's main attractions are the summer palaces and gardens at Sanssouci, built in the 18th and 19th centuries. The vast grounds are peppered with palaces, pavilions, fountains and temples. The park itself can be enjoyed for free, although, at the small vending machines by the entrances, a voluntary admission charge is requested, to help with maintenance.

Sanssouci Palace
Frederick the Great found the royal palace in Berlin not to his liking, so in 1744 commissioned Georg von Knobelsdorff to design **Schloss Sanssouci ❹** (Maulbeerallee; tel: 0331-969 4200;

Nov–Mar: Tue–Sun 10am–5pm, Apr–Oct: Tue–Sun 10am–6pm; park free; palace accessible by guided tour; charge) according to his (Frederick's) own sketches. Despite being single-storey, the palace is impressive, with a 97m (300ft) garden front, floor-to-ceiling windows and 35 huge caryatids supporting the roof and dome architrave.

Highlights of the rococo interior include the Konzertsaal (Concert Chamber), where the walls and ceiling are overlaid with a delicate gilt filigree and, at the centre of the palace (beneath the dome), the Marmorsaal (Marble Hall), which features exquisite Carrara marble columns and stucco

Food and Drink 🍴
① JULIETTE
Jägerstrasse 39; tel: 0331-270 1791; www.restaurant-juliette.de; noon-11pm; €€
This tiny, cosy traditional French restaurant in the heart of the Dutch quarter offers good-value delicious set menus, a great wine selection and warm service.

Babelsberg Film Studios
Cinemaphiles should make the short trip from Potsdam to Babelsberg for the Filmpark Babelsberg (Grossbeerenstrasse Potsdam; tel: 0331-721 2750; www.filmpark-babelsberg.de; daily 10am–6pm; charge). To get there, take the train from S-Bahn Potsdam-Stadt to S-Bahn Babelsberg. The film park incorporates the historic UFA film studios, where Marlene Dietrich, Greta Garbo and other German stars of the big screen started their careers. There's also the Filmmuseum Potsdam, housed in 17th-century military stables.

figures perched high on the cornice. Among the guest rooms, the yellow 'Voltaire' room *(see below)* boasts lavish rococo decoration including wooden parrots hanging from perches.

Picture Gallery and New Chambers

Buildings adjacent to the main palace include the **Bildergalerie** (Picture Gallery; tel: 0331-969 4181; www.spsg.de; May–Oct: Thur–Sun 10am–6pm; charge), designed to house Frederick's collection of paintings by masters such as Caravaggio and Rubens. It was the first building in Germany constructed specifically to house a museum.

Adjacent are the **Neue Kammern** (New Chambers; tel: 0331-969 4206; www.spsg.de; Apr: Sat, Sun 10am–6pm, May–Oct: Tue–Sun 10am–6pm;

charge), an orangery (1768) converted by Frederick into a guesthouse.

Chinese Teahouse

After seeing the main palace, you may like to enrol on a tour at the New Palace *(see below)*, Frederick's main residence, to the west. It can only be visited on a guided tour, however, so check your timing at the ticket office.

To get to the palace, walk down the beautifully terraced hill from Schloss Sanssouci, and turn right. This puts you onto the leafy Hauptallee.

En route, just off the Hauptallee, to the left, is the **Chinesisches Teehaus ❺** (Am Grünen Gitter; tel: 0331-969 4225; www.spsg.de; May–Oct: Tue–Sun 10am–6pm; charge), a whimsical gold-clad Chinese teahouse built from 1754 to 1757 and used for tea parties – the fine Chinese porcelain employed for that purpose is now on display here.

New Palace

At the western end of the Hauptallee is the largest palace at Sanssouci, the **Neues Palais ❻** (New Palace; tel: 0331-969 4202; Nov–Mar: Wed–Mon 10am–5pm, Apr–Oct: Wed–Mon 10am–6pm; www.spsg.de; charge), a vast structure built in the 1760s from red brick and white sandstone and covered in rococo statuary. It contains a rich collection of furniture, paintings by Italian, Dutch and French Baroque and rococo masters, and some fine 18th-century ceiling frescoes.

Frederick the Great

Frederick II made Prussia a military superpower, fought the bloody Seven Years War against Russia, Austria and France, and turned Potsdam into his personal playground. Estranged from his wife (whom he kept at a distance at Schloss Charlottenburg in Berlin – distinct from Sanssouci's Schloss Charlottenhof), he disliked Berlin and stayed at Sanssouci, with his beloved greyhounds, flute (he was an accomplished musician), French books and paintings. One of his closest companions was the French philosopher Voltaire, a regular visitor. Frederick is buried at the palace, next to his dogs, as he requested. His choice of name for the palace remains a mystery; meaning 'without worry, 'Sanssouci' can be taken to refer either to Frederick's motto or to his aspirations.

Other Highlights

Other highlights in the park include, in the southernmost corner, the small neoclassical **Schloss Charlottenhof** ❼ (Geschwister-Scholl-Strasse 34a; tel: 0331-969 4228; www.spsg.com; Tue–Sun 10am–6pm; charge), built by Schinkel for Crown Prince Frederick William IV. Adjacent are the Renaissance-style **Römische Bäder** (Roman Baths; tel: 0331-969 4225; www.spsg.de; end Apr–Oct: Tue–Sun 10am–6pm; charge),a complex comprising a tea pavilion, gardener's house, arcade hall and roman baths, also by Schinkel. Also notable, accessible via the path running to the northwest of the park, is the Italian Renaissance-style **Orangerie**, used as a hothouse. Near here is **Möven pick, see** ⑪②, the main option for refreshment at Sanssouci.

After you've seen all the sights within the park, either walk or catch the bus to return to **Potsdam Hauptbahnhof.** From here, you can take a train to central Berlin.

Potsdam Tourist Information

Branches of the above organisation can be found at Brandenburger Strasse 3, Potsdam, and at the Berlin-Infostore in Berlin HauptBahnhof station; tel: 0331-275 580; www.potsdam tourlsmus.de. For general information in English: www. potsdam.de. For details on Sanssouci park and its palaces, visit www.spsg.de.

Food and Drink 🍴

② POTSDAM HISTORISCHE MÜHLE (MÖVENPICK)
Zur Historischen Mühle 2; tel: 0331-281493; daily 8am–midnight; €€€
The Mövenpick restaurant is the only one right by Sanssouci Palace, so a choice of convenience above all else. It's light and airy, in a huge barn of a building, with large palm trees for decoration. In summer there's a beer garden and tables on the outdoor terrace. Meat-heavy menu. Children's menu too.

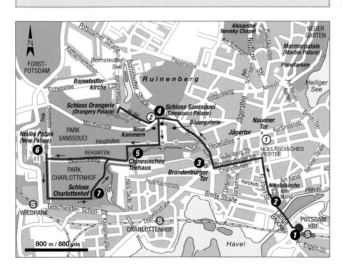

DIRECTORY

A user-friendly alphabetical listing of practical information, plus hand-picked hotels and restaurants, clearly organised by area, to suit all budgets and tastes. Select nightlife listings are also included here.

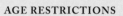

A

AGE RESTRICTIONS

The legal age to drink alcohol in Germany is 16. Cigarettes and other tobacco products can only be sold to adults over 18 years of age. The legal age for driving a car is 18, but most car-rental companies only allow drivers aged 21 and above to hire their vehicles (special insurance is required for those under 25).

B

BUDGETING

In general, Berlin is considerably more affordable than most large Western European cities. As a rule, a regular beer will cost you €3 and a glass of house wine €3–5. A main course at a budget eatery is around €10, at a moderate restaurant €12–20, and well above €25–30 in a top gourmet place. As for hotels, a room in a cheap one is around €50 per night, in a moderate one €90–120 and in a deluxe hotel anything from €150–200 and above. A taxi from Tegel airport to the central Western part of the city is €15–20 and €20–25 to the cental Eastern area. A taxi from Schönefeld airport will cost about €35–40 to the Ku'damm and around €30 to Unter den Linden. At time of printing, a single bus, tram or U-Bahn ticket, valid for two hours, cost €2.10.

If you are planning on doing lots of sightseeing, it may be worth investing in one of the Berlin Tourist Information service WelcomeCards. Valid for one adult and up to three children under the age of 14, these tourist passes include free use of public transport, and up to a 50 percent discount on many sights. They cover two, three or five days and cost €16.50 to €34.50. They are available from tourist offices, S-Bahn offices and some hotels.

Another good deal is the '3-Tage-Karte' museum pass, which gives access to all state museums for three consecutive days for €19. It can be purchased from any of the museums involved (see www.smb.spk-berlin.de for details).

C

CHILDREN

Berlin is relatively child-friendly – for a big city. As a rule, children under 12, 14 or 16 are given discounts on many admission fees. Further information on visiting Berlin with children can be found online at www.kinder-berlin.de.

CLOTHING

Berliners tend to dress less formally than Germans in general. Even in the evenings, most upmarket restaurants, cafés and bars do not have dress codes. While spring and summer can be nice and warm, the weather can be a little inclement, so bring a jumper, rain clothes and an umbrella. In winter, scarves, hats, gloves and other warm-weather gear, as well as waterproof footwear, are essential.

CRIME AND SAFETY

Street crime is rare in Berlin, and theft is usually limited to pickpocketing. However, visitors should observe the normal safety precautions: when sitting at a street café, don't leave your purse or handbag on a table or chair, and be vigilant on busy buses or trains. In some areas such as Kreuzberg's Kottbusser Tor, drug trafficking is a problem, but tourists are not usually targeted.

CUSTOMS

There are no customs restrictions on travellers from European Union (EU) countries, although they are also not eligible for VAT return. Visitors from outside the EU should observe their countries' individual regulations. When bringing in or taking out more than €10,000 in cash to or from Germany, the amount has to be registered with customs. Non-EU visitors can claim back VAT. Return forms are available at most large shops and department stores and should be handed in when you leave the country. German VAT on most goods is 19 percent (just 7 percent on books, flowers and transport).

D

DISABLED TRAVELLERS

For disabled travellers, Berlin is surprisingly well equipped. Almost all S- and U-Bahn stations have lifts, and all metros and regional trains have ramps (go to the first coach and alert the driver, who will assist you). On buses, the rear entrance usually has a lowerable ramp.

The following institutions can also offer help and advice:
Berliner Behindertenverband, tel: 030-204 3847.
Behindertenbeauftragter des Landes Berlin, tel: 030-9028 2917.
Deutscher Service Ring e.V., tel: 030-859 4010.

E

ELECTRICITY

In Germany, electricity is set at 220/230 volts. US and UK travellers will need adaptors and possibly a transformer.

EMBASSIES/CONSULATES

Australia: Wallstrasse 76–9; tel: 030-880 0880.
Canada: Leipziger Platz 17; tel: 030-203 120.
Ireland: Friedrichstrasse 200; tel: 030-220 720.
UK: Wilhelmstrasse 70; tel: 030-204 570.

Above from far left: children will love a visit to the zoo.

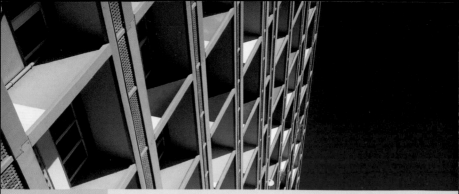

Above: Berlin's 1950s' Le Corbusier building, in Charlottenburg.

US: Pariser Platz 2; tel: 030-83050. US Consular Services at Clayallee 170.

EMERGENCIES

Ambulance and **Fire**: tel: 112
Police: tel: 110

In addition, the following are Berlin-based services: **DRK Ambulance,** tel: 030-850 055; **Ambulance,** tel: 030-3100 3222; **Narcotics and Drugs Emergencies,** tel: 030-19237; **Helpline International,** tel: 030-4401 0607.

FESTIVALS/FAIRS

January
Internationale Grüne Woche (International Green Week; www.gruene woche.de)

February
Berlinale (Berlin Film Festival; www.berlinale.de)
ITB (International Tourism Fair; www.itb-berlin.de)

March
Karneval der Kulturen
(Cultural Carnival; www.karneval-berlin.de)

May/Early June
DKB-ISTAF
(International track-and-field event; www.istaf.de)

June
Luft- und Raumfahrtsausstellung Berlin Brandenburg (Air and Space fair; www.ila-berlin.de)
Christopher Street Day (gay street parade; www.csd-berlin.de)
Deutsch-Französisches Volksfest (German/French Folk Festival)

July
Open Air Classic (www.classicopen air.de)
Deutsch-Amerikanisches Volksfest (German/American Folk Festival; www.deutsch-amerikanisches-volksfest.de)
Internationale Funkaustellung (International entertainment and music fair; www.ifa-berlin.de)

September
Popkomm (International pop music fair and festival; www.popkomm.de)
Berlin Marathon (www.berlin-mara thon.de; last weekend of month)

October
Tag der Deutschen Einheit (Day of German Unity; 3 Oct)
Jazz Fest Berlin
(www.berliner-festspiele.de)

November
Weihnachtsmärkte
(Christmas markets; www.weihnachts markt-deutschland.de/berlin.html)

December
Christmas

FURTHER READING

Many novels have been written about Berlin. To dive into the heydays of the Jazz Age in the shadow of Fascism, turn to Christopher Isherwood's *Berlin Diaries. Berlin, Alexanderplatz: The Story of Franz Biberkopf (see p.58)* by Alfred Döblin is the archetypical Berlin novel. *Berlin* by David Clay Large and the more dramatic *Faust's Metropolis* by Alexandra Richie are good introductions to the city's history. Antony Beevor's *Fall of Berlin 1945* chronicles the last days of World War II, while *The Berlin Wall: A World Divided* by Frederick Taylor tells the story of a city divided and then resurrected.

G

GAY AND LESBIAN ISSUES

With an estimated gay and lesbian population of 300,000 people and an openly gay mayor, Berlin has one of the world's most vibrant gay communities. The gay scene is not exclusive to any one district, but most of the nightlife action can be found around Nollendorfplatz in Schöneberg, as well as in Kreuzberg and Prenzlauer Berg.

GREEN ISSUES

Germans are devoted environmentalists, and in most public buildings, and even in hotels, you will see a seriously organised separation of rubbish. In Berlin, 'green' transport is readily available by renting bikes under the Deutsche Bahn (DB) 'Call a Bike' scheme *(see right)* or by taking a bike rickshaw, or 'Velotaxi'. The latter wait for passengers at the Brandenburg Gate, the Reichstag, outside KaDeWe, and on Breitscheidplatz.

H

HEALTH

Healthcare and Insurance

Visitors from the UK should obtain a European Health Insurance Card (EHIC) from post offices or online (see www.ehic.org.uk for more information) before travelling to Germany. This entitles them to free emergency healthcare, but note that it does not give any cover for trip cancellations, nor does it provide repatriation in case of illness. North American visitors should take out private health insurance before travelling to Germany.

Hospitals and Pharmacies

German doctors and hospital staff mostly speak English very well, and Berlin is blessed with several state-of-the-art university clinics and high-standard public hospitals. Pharmacies in each district rotate for late-night services, with details of the nearest night service posted in their windows.

Above: rental bikes – part of Deutsche Bahn's Call a Bike scheme. Register your personal details (including a credit or debit card) on the web at www.callabike.de or call tel: 07000-522 5522. You'll be given a customer number, and a small sum (around €5) will be debited from your account. Once you've registered, you're ready to ride. To access the code to the lock of a bike, call or text DB using the number in the red box on the cover of the lock. You then type the number in on the display underneath the cover. Once you've finished with the bike, lock it either to a traffic sign or a bike stand at a major crossroads and close the lock. When the display reads 'Return Bike', hit 'Yes'. You'll be given a receipt code, which you need to give over the phone to the Call a Bike centre, along with the bike's location.

HOURS AND HOLIDAYS

In general, shops and offices open for business Monday to Friday from 9 or 10am to 6 or 8pm. On Saturday, many larger stores remain open until 8pm, while smaller shops close early, at 2 or 4pm. All shops are shut on Sunday. Banks usually open from 9 or 10am until 4 or 6pm; most banks close on one afternoon a week, usually Wednesday or Friday. Post offices open Monday to Saturday, 8am–6pm.

National and Religious Holidays

The list below shows the public holidays celebrated in Berlin, when shops, banks, official departments and many restaurants are closed.

1 Jan: New Year's Day (Neujahrstag).
Mar/Apr: Good Friday; Easter Sunday; Easter Monday (Ostern).
1 May: Labour Day.
40 days after Easter: Ascension (Christi Himmelfahrt).
May/June: Whit Monday (Pfingsten).
3 Oct: Day of German Unity (Tag der Deutschen Einheit).
25, 26 Dec: Christmas Day and Boxing Day (Weihnachten). Note that on 24 Dec (Christmas Eve) shops stay open until noon, but most restaurants, theatres, cinemas and concert halls close.

If a holiday falls on a Thursday, many people take the Friday off to make a long weekend.

I

INTERNET FACILITIES

Berlin has quite a few internet cafés, mostly in Charlottenburg, Kreuzberg and Mitte. There are internet cafés in many of the main stations, including the Ostbahnhof, Alexanderplatz S-Bahn station, Zoologischer Garten S-Bahn and opposite the main entrance to Bahnhof Zoo.

L

LANGUAGE

General Words and Phrases

yes *ja*
no *nein*
maybe *vielleicht*
please *bitte*
thank you *danke*
you're welcome *gern geschehen*
hi/hello *Hallo*
Good morning *Guten Morgen*
Good evening *Guten Abend*
Goodbye *Auf Wiedersehen*
See you tomorrow *bis morgen*
I'm looking for... *Ich suche…*
Where is…? *Wo ist…?*
What is…? *Was ist…?*
When is…? *Wann ist…?*
What is your name?
Wie heisst du? (informal)
Wie heissen Sie? (formal)
My name is... *Ich heisse...*
How are you? *Wie geht es Ihnen?*

I'm fine, and you?
Mir geht es gut, und Ihnen?
I'm... *Ich bin...*
I don't understand *Ich verstehe nicht*
I understand *Ich verstehe*
I don't know *Ich weiss nicht*
Can you repeat?
Können Sie das wiederholen?
I'm sorry *Es tut mir leid*
Excuse me *Verzeihung*
Where are the toilets?
Wo sind die Toiletten?
Ladies/Gentlemen *Damen/Herren*
free *kostenlos*
here *hier*
there *dort*
right/left *rechts/links*
straight on *geradeaus*
upstairs *oben*
downstairs *unten*
near/far *nah/weit*
opposite *gegenüber*
beside *neben*
today/tomorrow *heute/morgen*
now/late *jetzt/später*
open/closed *geöffnet/geschlossen*
Help! *Hilfe!*
street *die Strasse*
palace *das Schloss*
church *die Kirche*

On Arrival
How do I get to...?
Wie komme ich zu...?
I want to get off at...
Ich möchte aussteigen...
How far is it? *Wie weit ist es?*
departure/arrival *Abfahrt/Ankunft*

train station *der Bahnhof*
bus stop *die Bushaltestelle*
train *der Zug*
car *das Auto*
ticket *der Fahrschein*
return ticket *die Rückfahrkarte*
platform *der Bahnsteig*
city map *der Stadtplan*
I'd like to change money
Ich möchte Geld wechseln
I'd like a single room/double room
*Ich möchte ein Einzelzimmer/
Doppelzimmer*
with bathroom *mit Bad*
Please show me another room
Bitte zeigen Sie mir ein anderes Zimmer
Is breakfast included?
Mit Frühstück?
to book *reservieren*
lift *Fahrstuhl*
key *Schlüssel*

Eating Out
I would like to...
Ich möchte einen Tisch
...reserve a table for four
für vier Personen bestellen
What do you recommend?
Was empfehlen Sie?
breakfast *Frühstück*
lunch *Mittagessen*
dinner *Abendessen*
the menu *die Karte*
Do you have vegetarian dishes?
Haben Sie vegetarische gerichte?
The bill, please *Die Rechnung, bitte*
We'd like separate bills
Wir möchten getrennt bezahlen

Above from far
left: friendly sign
at the traffic lights;
Grosse (Große)
Hamburger Strasse.

together *zusammen*
change *Wechselgeld*

Shopping
shop *der Laden, das Geschäft*
department store *das Kaufhaus*
I'm just browsing
Ich schaue mich nur um
I'd like to buy…
Ich möchte kaufen...
Do you have… *Haben Sie…*
How much is it? *Was kostet das?*
a different size *eine andere Grösse*
Do you take credit cards?
Nehmen Sie Kreditkarten?

Health
doctor *der Arzt*
dentist *der Zahnarzt*
hospital *das Krankenhaus*
pharmacy *die Apotheke*
prescription *Rezept*
I'm sick *Ich bin krank*
It's an emergency *Es ist ein Notfall*
police *Polizei*
What is your mobile (phone) number?
Was ist deine Handynummer?

LOST PROPERTY

Berlin's central bureau for lost property
is the **Zentrales Fundbüro**, Platz der
Luftbrücke 6; tel: 030-7560 3101. If
you lose something on a bus, tram or
U-Bahn, contact: **BVG**, Potsdamer
Strasse 180–2; Mon–Thur 9am–6pm,
Fri 9am–2pm; tel: 030-19449. For lug-
gage lost on an S-Bahn or Deutsche
Bahn train, contact the **Zentrales
Fundbüro der Deutschen Bahn AG**
on tel: 0900-199 0599.

M

MAPS

Excellent free city maps are available
in tourist information offices and in
some larger hotels. Free public transport maps are available at S- and
U-Bahn stations.

MEDIA

Print Media
Among the nine daily newspapers available in Berlin, the local *Der Tagesspiegel*
and the *Berliner Zeitung* offer the best-
quality news, insightful cultural reviews
and good local coverage. Other papers
include the more business-orientated
Die Welt and the down-to-earth *Berliner
Morgenpost*, while the irreverent left-
wing *taz* (Berlin *Tageszeitung)* is
entertaining to read if you speak good
enough German. The two biggest-
selling tabloid papers are the local
Berliner Zeitung (BZ) and the noto-
riously scandalous national, *Bild*.
Tagesspiegel, *Berliner Zeitung* and
Berliner Morgenpost have special-event
calendars on Wednesday or Thursday.

In terms of city listings magazines,
the most prominent ones are *tip* and
zitty, both published bimonthly. The
monthly *Prinz* offers information for a

young, party-orientated crowd, as does the even funkier *030* (named after the Berlin dialling code). The only English-language magazine is the monthly *Exberliner (*www.exberliner.de).

Radio

You can get up-to-date national and local news in German on the news-only InfoRadio (FM93.1). For the news and other programmes in English, tune in to the BBC World Service (FM 90.2).

Television

In Germany there are two national television channels – ARD and ZDF – plus regional stations and several private and cable stations. The BBC, CNN, CNBC, Bloomberg TV, France 2, TV 5 and MTV are usually available in medium-priced to luxury hotels.

MONEY

Currency

In common with most other EU countries, the euro (€) is the official currency used in Germany. Notes are denominated in 5, 10, 20, 50, 100 and 500 euros; coins in 1 and 2 euros and 1, 2, 5, 10, 20 and 50 cents.

Credit Cards

Rather surprisingly to Western and North American travellers, credit cards are not as widely accepted in Berlin as they are in many other international

destinations. Many shops, smaller restaurants and bars, pubs, small theatres, etc, will not accept them at all; some smaller places accept them only for larger amounts. Keep some cash on you at all times, just in case.

Where credit cards are accepted, American Express, Diners, MasterCard and Visa are the most usual ones.

Cash Machines

Cash machines can be found across Berlin, mostly in banks and post offices, but also in department stores and stations. You will rarely find cash machines in grocery or convenience stores or smaller shops of any kind.

Travellers' Cheques

Travellers' cheques are only accepted in hotels, department stores and tourist-orientated restaurants.

Tipping

As far as tipping in restaurants is concerned, Berliners tend to add on an extra 10 percent for service. Standard cover or service charges are not typical. Do not simply leave your tip *(Trinkgeld)* on the table, however – hand it directly to the waiter. When tipping in hotels or taxis, simply round up the amount to the next euro or so.

Taxes

German sales tax (VAT) is currently levelled at 19 percent on most products. It is always included in the prices

Above from far left: newspapers hanging up in a café; checking the map.

you see on a price tag or on the menu. The VAT on newspapers, books, pet food and transport is just 7 percent. There are no special city, tourist or hotel taxes in Berlin.

POLICE

The emergency telephone number for the police is tel: 110. In Berlin, you will see regular German police (wearing green uniform jackets and beige trousers) and Federal police (in dark-blue uniforms).

POST

Germany's Deutsche Post is the country's only mail carrier, covering all mail and post services. Post offices can be found throughout Berlin and can be recognised by a black bugle on a bright yellow background. Post offices usually open Monday to Friday 8am to 6pm and Saturday 8am to noon. Only a handful of larger Berlin post offices have longer opening hours. These include:

- **Joachimstaler Strasse 7**: Mon–Sat 8am–midnight, Sun 10am–10pm.
- **Tegel airport**: Mon–Fri 8am–6pm, Sat 8am–1pm.
- **S-Bahn Friedrichstrasse**: Mon–Fri 6am–10pm, Sat–Sun 8am–10pm.

Information on other postal services can be found at: www.deutschepost.de.

Stamps and Postboxes

At time of printing, a stamp *(eine Brief-marke)* for a postcard to the UK cost €0.65 and €0.70 for a letter. The normal delivery time is about 3 to 5 days. A stamp for an airmail letter to the US cost €1.70 and for a postcard €1. Delivery takes at least 5 days.

Postboxes are bright yellow, and, if there is more than one slot, you should deposit non-local letters or cards in the slot marked *Andere Postleitzahlen (PLZ)*.

RELIGION

Berlin is an overwhelmingly Protestant city, with large Catholic, Muslim and Jewish communities. In general, religious tolerance is quite high in Berlin, despite some sad but insular incidents against Jewish citizens or visitors.

A complete list of churches, synagogues, mosques and temples can be obtained from the tourist office *(see opposite)*.

S

SMOKING

Smoking is strictly prohibited in all public buildings and institutions as well as on public transport and related stations. Smoking is also banned in pubs, restaurants and clubs – a law that

is strictly enforced, as owners and guests have to pay hefty fines when not in compliance. The only exceptions are restaurants or pubs that offer separate smokers' rooms.

T

TELEPHONES

Germany country code: 49
Berlin area code: 030 (note that you do not have to dial this code when inside the code area of the city itself)
Potsdam area code: 0331

For international calls, dial 00 plus the country code and then the area code (without the intial '0'), then the number.

Communications within Germany and to neighbouring countries are cheaper from 6pm to 8am weekdays and all day Saturday and Sunday. Rates for Canada and the US are cut between midnight and noon.

Country Codes
Australia: 61
Canada: 1
Ireland: 353
New Zealand: 64
UK: 44
US: 1

Operator Numbers
You can reach the national operator ('Auskunft') on tel: 11833 (no area code) and the international operator on tel: 11834 (no area code).

Mobile (Cell) Phones
All major mobile phone firms, including O2, T-Mobile and Vodafone, operate in Germany.

Card Phones
Although some public phone boxes are still coin-operated, those accepting phone cards *(Telefonkarten)* are increasingly common, and there are some that also accept credit cards. Phone cards can be obtained at post offices and in many kiosks.

TIME ZONES

Germany follows Central European Time (GMT +1). When it is noon in Berlin, it is 11 am in London and 6am in New York City.

TOILETS

Public toilets are readily found in Berlin and are typically fairly clean. Always have small change ready in case the door has a coin slot. Toilets may be labelled with symbols of a man or a woman or the initials WC, or else with 'Herren' (Gentlemen) or 'Damen' (Ladies).

TOURIST INFORMATION

In Berlin
The Berlin Tourist Office – Berlin Tourismus Marketing GmbH (BTM) – is responsible for promoting and organising tourism in the city. It has

Above from far left: for international post, use the slot in the postbox labelled 'Andere Postleitzahlen' (other postage costs); cross on the Berliner Dom.

Alexanderplatz

an excellent website, www.visitBerlin. de, which is good for hotel and ticket bookings and further information on the city. It also has a central tourist hotline: tel: 030-250 025.

It runs several centrally located 'Berlin Infostores' in the city. These can be found at:

Hauptbahnhof (Central Train Station): ground level, entrance at Europaplatz; daily 8am–10pm.

Neues Kranzler-Eck: Kurfürstendamm 21; Mon–Sat 10am–8pm, Sun 10am–6pm (longer opening hours Apr–Oct).

Brandenburger Tor: Southern Gatehouse, Pariser Platz; daily 10am–6pm (longer from Apr to Oct).

ALEXA Shopping Centre: Grunerstrasse 20; ground level; Mon–Sat 10am–8pm (longer from Apr to Oct).

In addition to free maps, lists and brochures, Berlin's tourist offices sell WelcomeCards *(see p.96)* and tickets for museums, the theatre and other events across the city.

German Tourist Offices Abroad

The German National Tourist Board also maintains offices in many countries throughout the world:

Canada: 480 University Avenue, Suite 1500, Toronto, Ontario M5G IV2; tel: 416-968 1685.

UK: PO Box 2695, London W1A 3TN; tel: 020-7317 0908.

US: 122 East 42nd Street, New York, NY 10168-0072; tel: 212-661 7200; 1334 Parkview Avenue, Suite 300, Manhattan Beach, CA 90266; tel: 310-545 1350.

TOURS AND GUIDES

Boat Tours

Apart from regular walking and bus sightseeing tours, Berlin offers a great many speciality guided tours, including boat trips along its canals and lakes. Most tours are 3 to 4 hours long and start at the Schloss Charlottenburg or the Schlossbrücke, by Museum Island. Firms running boat tours include: **Reederei Bruno Winkler**; Mierendorffstrasse 16; tel: 030-349 9595; www.reedereiwinkler. de; and **Stern und Kreis Schifffahrt**; Puschkinallee 16; tel: 030-536 3600; www.sternundkreis.de.

Bunker Tours

Tours through bunkers and forgotten underground areas of Berlin are offered by: **Berliner Unterwelten e.V.;** Brunnenstrasse 105; tel: 030-4606 8956; www.berliner-unterwelten.de.

TRANSPORT

Airports and Arrival

Berlin currently has two airports, Tegel (TXL) in northern Charlottenburg, and Schönefeld (SXF), 24km (15 miles) southeast of Berlin. Schönefeld is currently being expanded *(see opposite)*, and Tegel will close by the time the new Schönefeld is fully open. The historic city airport Tempelhof *(see*

p. 80) shut down in late 2008. Information on both Berlin airports is available at www.berlin-airport.de and on tel: 0180-500 0186.

While direct flights from all major European destinations fly into and out of Berlin, there are only a handful of transcontinental flights. If you travel to Berlin from the US (except from New York, which is served by direct flights), your most likely connection will be through either Frankfurt, Munich or Düsseldorf or another European city.

Tegel Airport

Tegel airport, currently used mostly for non-budget airlines, is located some 6km (4 miles) from the city centre. The best way into the city is by the express bus to the bus station in front of Bahnhof Zoologischer Garten or by TXL Jetexpress bus, which runs from the airport to Unter den Linden and Alexanderplatz. Buses leave regularly and take about half an hour; the fare is around €3, or an additional €1 if you already have a standard U-Bahn or bus ticket. Alternatively, you can take bus 109 to Jakob-Kaiser-Platz and change to the subway (U7). A taxi from Tegel to the Ku'damm is around €15–20, and to East Berlin about €25–30.

Schönefeld Airport

Located about 19km (12 miles) south-east of the city centre, Schönefeld is currently used mainly for holiday flights, low-budget flights with airlines such as easyJet and Ryanair, and flights to Eastern Europe and Asia, but it is being expanded to create a new regional airport (Airport Berlin Brandenburg International; BBI; www.berlin-airport.de) for the capital. This is scheduled for completion in 2011.

The fastest way to get into the city from Schönefeld is the Airport-Express rail link, which takes 28 minutes to Alexanderplatz, the Hauptbahnhof and Bahnhof Zoo. (A free shuttle bus runs between the airport and the S-Bahn Flughafen Schönefeld station; bus 171 also runs to the station.) The S-Bahn also runs into the city centre from S-Bahn Flughafen Schönefeld. Bus 171 connects the airport to the nearest U-Bahn station: Rudow. If you want to take a taxi, expect to pay at least €35 to reach West Berlin, and about €30 to get to East Berlin.

Public Transport

The city's extensive network of U-Bahn, S-Bahn, commuter trains, trams and buses is fairly easy to navigate, comfortable, pretty punctual and quite safe. All the modes of transport above are part of the same system, so you can switch between them with the same ticket. The city of Berlin and its surroundings are divided into three fare zones: A, B and C (going from the city centre to the outlying areas). For the most part, you will only need AB-combined tickets.

For single rides, there are two tickets, the 'Kurzstrecke' (€1.30), allowing you to ride three stops in one direction, and a standard ticket (€2.10), allowing you to take any form of public transport in one direction within a period of two hours. Returning to the original station and making round trips are not allowed.

If you're planning on making a few journeys, it pays to buy a travelcard. Options for this include 'Tageskarten' (Day Cards), which allow unlimited access for day (AB zone: €6.10) until 3am. Another possibility is a Welcome Card *(see p.96)*, which includes free use of public transport, and up to a 50 per-cent discount on many sights.

If you are travelling as a group, a 'Kleingruppenkarte' (Small Group Card) is a good deal. This allows up to five individuals to travel together for a whole day for €15.40 to €16.10, depending on the number of zones covered. A Sieben-Tages-Karte (Seven Day Card) is valid for a week and costs between €26.20 (AB zones) and €32.30 (ABC zones).

All tickets can be bought in stations and on buses and trams. They must be stamped at the start of your journey in the red or yellow box at platform entrances or at bus stops. Fines for not doing so are steep.

S- and U-Bahn trains usually run daily until midnight or 1am; on Fridays, Saturday and nights prior to public holidays, the yellow metro and the red S-Bahn trains operate throughout the night. An extensive network of night buses operates daily every night.

The city also has trams, although these are found mostly in the eastern districts. Special 'M' lines of buses or trams are operate in areas with few U-Bahn lines.

U-Bahn and S-Bahn lines run every 2 to 10 minutes, depending on the time of day. Commuter trains, buses and trams run slightly less frequently.

Taxis

Berlin's taxis are a little hit or miss: some drivers are very friendly and know the city well, offering an excel-lent service and lovely clean cars (mostly Mercedes), while others are not as communicative or knowledgeable.

You can hail a taxi on the street or at a taxi rank, or call one on one of these central call-centre numbers: tel: 030-261 026/030-210 101/030-443 322. Note that you are supposed always to take the first taxi in line – this isn't a legal requirement, more a local custom, and you'll make the drivers angry if you don't abide by it.

When hailing a taxi on the street, and only travelling a short way, you can ask for a 'Kurzstreckentarif' (short-dis-tance rate), which is just €3.50 for 2km (1¼ miles). Taxi fares are calculated by the kilometre, with extra charges for waiting times, journeys taken at night or at the weekend, and for luggage.

Driving

Driving a car by yourself in Berlin is relatively straightforward, but be aware that Germans tend to be fast drivers, and Berliners, in particular, drive quite aggressively. The speed limit within the city is usually 50km/h (30 miles per hour), but an increasing number of streets have speed restrictions of just 30km/h (18 miles per hour), the latter being keenly observed by locals and the police.

Drink-driving with an alcohol level of more than 0.8 percent is a serious offence and involves hefty fines and extremely serious repercussions in case of an accident. The Berlin police often set up checkpoints on weekend nights.

Car Hire

Hiring a car is fairly easy in Germany – you just to be over a certain age *(see p.96)*, have a driver's licence, passport and credit card. Pre-booking a car before you travel is always cheaper than trying to hire one on the spot. On Fridays, in particular, it can be difficult to find a car free to rent in Berlin.

Car-rental firms with offices in Berlin include:

Avis: Tegel airport: tel: 030-4101 3148. Budapester Strase 43 (Europa Center); tel: 030-230 9370.

Europcar: Tegel airport; tel: 030-417 8520. Omnibusbahnhof, Messedamm 8; tel: 030-306 9590.

Hertz: Tegel airport; tel: 030-4170 4674. Budapester Strasse 39; tel: 030-261 1053.

Sixt: Tegel airport; tel: 030-4101 2886. Budapester Strasse 45; tel: 030-4101 2886.

V

VISAS AND PASSPORTS

Visitors from the EU, the US, Canada and Australia don't need a visa for visiting Germany, just a valid national identity card (EU citizens) or a passport (with at least three months left to run on it). Visitors from other countries need a valid passport and should check regulations with their local German Consulate.

W

WEBSITES

In addition to the many websites included throughout this book, useful sites are: www.berlin.de (the official website of the city and state of Berlin); www.btm.de (visitor-orientated city site); and www.berlinonline.de (event website; also represents the *tip* listings magazine and the daily local newspaper the *Berliner Zeitung*).

WEIGHTS AND MEASURES

The metric system is used in Germany.

WOMEN

Female travellers should feel very safe in Berlin. However, as anywhere, it's wise to exercise caution when alone at night, especially on public transport.

Above from far left: taxi sign; an unusually quiet station.

On average, Berlin's hotels tend to be cheaper than in other Western European cities, except during major festivals and fairs such as the Berlinale in February or the IFA (Consumer Electronics Show) in September. At the lower end, the best places to look are Mitte, Prenzlauer Berg and Kreuzberg; also recommended are old-fashioned 'Pensionen' (B&Bs). At the top end of the scale, the city has a growing number of luxury hotels, mostly around Unter den Linden and off Gendarmenmarkt.

Charlottenburg

Hotel Q!

Knesebeckstrasse 33–4; tel: 030-8182 5720; www.loock-hotels.com; U: Uhlandstrasse, S: Savignyplatz; €€
One of Berlin's coolest hotels, the Q is legendary for attracting Hollywood stars who want to avoid the paparazzi. It's so hip, in fact, that the nondescript, modern building doesn't even have a sign outside. Designed in futuristic style, it is surprisingly comfortable, with a playfulness that belies its aesthetics, such as a bath that can be rolled into from the bed. There is also a fantastic on-site spa and a super-chic bar and restaurant.

Price for a double room for one night without breakfast:	
€€€€	over 350 euros
€€€	200–350 euros
€€	120–200 euros
€	below 120 euros

Ku'damm 101 Hotel

Kurfürstendamm 101; tel: 030-520 0550; www.kudamm101.com; U: Adenauerplatz, S: Halensee; €–€€
This small, well-designed, minimalist hotel is on the western section of the Ku'damm. Despite the busy location, the rooms are quiet – they're small, with basic amenities, but the beds are comfortable and the bathrooms are neatly designed with a light touch of 1980s retro chic. Amenities include WiFi access, a spa and a rooftop breakfast room with nice views.

Pension Dittberner

Wielandstrasse 26; tel: 030-881 6485; www.hotel-dittberner.de; U: Adenauerplatz or Uhlandstrasse, S: Savignyplatz; €
This old-fashioned 'Pension' is housed in a late 19th-century mansion off the Ku'damm. It's a maze of high-ceilinged rooms with creaky parquet floors. It's a stylistic mish-mash, but the charming staff and the historic atmosphere more than compensate.

Propeller Island City Lodge

Albrecht-Achilles-Strasse 58; tel: 030-891 9016; www.propeller-island.com; U: Adenauerplatz, S: Charlottenburg; €–€€
The City Lodge is an eccentric self-described 'habitable work of art in the heart of Berlin', designed by owner and concept artist Lard Stroschen. No two rooms are alike. Get inspired amid sur-

real colours, slanted floors, 'sound sculptures' and suspended beds. Alternatively, you can sleep in a coffin, a cage or a prison cell. Not all rooms have full bathrooms. There are no traditional reception services or a restaurant – not a problem since the lodge is just a block away from the Ku'damm. Good service.

Savoy Hotel

Fasanenstrasse 9–10; tel: 030-311 030; www.hotel-savoy.com; U+S: Zoologischer Garten; €€

This classy old-style hotel on Fasanenstrasse (a pretty historic side street just off the Ku'damm) has a proud history, with Greta Garbo and Thomas Mann both on its past guest list. The comfortable rooms are classically designed. Facilities include a smoking club (La Casa del Habano), an in-house restaurant – the smart, traditionally furnished, scarlet-painted Weinrot, which does a great lunch buffet – and an inviting courtyard.

Tiergarten

Intercontinental Berlin

Budapester Strasse 2; tel: 030-26020; www.ichotelsgroup.com; U: Wittenbergplatz, U+S: Zoologischer Garten; €€€

At first glance, the well-established five-star Interconti may remind you of an airport, with its huge lobby. But the service is much more personal than might expected from a hotel on this scale. The renovated rooms, with tra-

ditional furnishings, are huge and offer sweeping views of the Tiergarten. The ones in the east wing are the most attractively decorated. Facilities include a café and Hugo's *(see p.41)*.

Potsdamer Platz

Grand Hyatt Berlin

Marlene-Dietrich-Platz 2; tel: 030-2553 1234; www.berlin.grand.hyatt.com; U+S: Potsdamer Platz; €€€

The official hotel of the Berlinale film festival, in a great location right on Marlene-Dietrich-Platz, the Hyatt is known for its smooth, personal service, the über-stylish Vox bar and restaurant and stylish, minimalist rooms, with well-designed features. The standard rates are generally high, but the hotel often has special weekend or other promotional offers.

The Mandala Hotel

Potsdamer Strasse 3; tel: 030-5900 50000; www.themandala.de; U+S: Potsdamer Platz; €€€–€€€€

The rooms in this upmarket four-star hotel near Potsdamer Platz are all suites, with beautifully elegant contemporary decor. Facilities include the Michelin-starred Facil restaurant and a great spa.

Mitte

Dorint Sofitel am Gendarmenmarkt

Charlottenstrasse 50–2; tel: 030-203 750; www.sofitel.com; U: Französiche Strasse or Stadtmitte; €€

Above from far left: spa at the Hotel Q!; room at the Grand Hyatt.

Public Transport
Note that in the practical information for each entry we quote the nearest U-Bahn (U) or S-Bahn (S) station.

This well-established classic off Gendarmenmarkt is a hidden gem among the flashier luxury hotels in this area. The service is friendly and the Austrian restaurant Aigner a delight. The rooms offer great views of the neoclassical square.

Honigmond Hotel

Tieckstrasse 12; tel: 030-284 4550; www.honigmond-berlin.de; U: Zinnowitzer Strasse, S: Nordbahnhof; €€–€€€

The Honigmond is an insider's secret. Beautifully restored, it occupies a traditional tenement block and offers individually designed rooms. There's also a separate house, dating to 1845, which boasts a pretty, leafy courtyard. Surprisingly quiet given the hotel's location, which is excellent for the local nightlife.

Hotel Adlon Kempinski Berlin

Unter den Linden 77; tel: 030-22610; www.hotel-adlon.de; S: Unter den Linden; €€€€

Probably Berlin's most famous address since it went up in 1907, the Adlon has paid host to scores of luminaries, from the crowned heads of Europe to Thomas Edison, Albert Einstein and Charlie Chaplin. Readers of Isherwood's *Berlin Stories* will recognise the name, and it was here that Marlene Dietrich was discovered. In 1945, having survived the war, it was destroyed by an accidental fire, and

although parts of it remained, it was finally demolished in 1984. After reunification, the building was rebuilt from original plans, and the new Adlon opened its doors in 1997. Its many rooms are some of the most luxurious in the city and have prices to match, but no other Berlin hotel offers a view of the Brandenburg Gate and such quick access to Berlin's cultural centres.

Hotel de Rome Berlin

Behrenstrasse 37; tel: 030-460 6090; www.hotelderome.de; U: Französische Strasse, S: Friedrichstrasse; €€€€

British hotelier Sir Rocco Forte opened this hotel in a 19th-century former bank in the historic Forum Fridericianum, close to the State Opera. The hotel has a breathtaking spa (incorporating an old walk-in safe) and good-sized contemporary-style rooms.

Lux Eleven

Rosa-Luxemburg-Strasse 9–13; tel: 030-936 2800; www.lux-eleven.com; U+S: Alexanderplatz, U: Rosa-Luxemburg-Platz; €€

This luxurious contemporary design hotel in a restored tenement block in northern Mitte is a great choice for stylish visitors. The rooms are very airy and bright, with all-white decor or touches in muted browns. Top-notch facilities include an Aveda hair salon and the sleekly designed Asian Shiro i Shiro restaurant *(see p.116).*

Die Fabrik

Schlesische Strasse 18; tel: 030-611
7116; www.diefabrik.com; U: Schlesisches Tor; €

This hostel offers great value in the
heart of the vibrant Kreuzberg district
with myriad bars, cafés and nightlife
options at your fingertips. There are
shared bathrooms and no lift, televisions
or telephones in the rooms, or credit
cards accepted, but this hostel is ideal for
backpackers, families, groups or individuals on a budget. Housed in a converted
red-brick factory building, the quiet and
clean rooms (shared) are basic but cosy,
with wooden floors and rugs.

Hotel Riehmer's Hofgarten

Yorckstrasse 83; tel: 030-78098800;
www.hotel-riehmers-hofgarten.de; U:
Mehringdamm, S: Yorckstrasse; €€
This hotel is a little off the beaten track,
but it's one of the most historic in the
city, set in a fine neoclassical 19th-cen-
tury mansion in the heart of Kreuzberg.
The friendly service, contemporary interior decor, E.T.A. Hoffmann restaurant
(see p.81) and an upmarket international
clientele add to the appeal.

Mövenpick Hotel Kreuzberg

Schöneberger Strasse 3; tel: 030-
230 060; www.moevenpick-hotels.
com; S: Anhalter Bahnhof; €-€€
The Mövenpick is a welcoming business
hotel, with some design pretensions, in
a large historic building (the salmon-

pink façade is unmissable) in Kreuzberg,
just near the Anhalter Bahnhof and
Checkpoint Charlie. The large, modern
rooms are smart and in the modern
style; the ones under the roof have the
most character. The large restaurant
does a tasty, well-priced lunch buffet.
Good service.

Ackselhaus Berlin

Belforter Strasse 21; tel: 030-4433
7633; www.ackselhaus.de; U: Senefelder Platz; €€
This boarding house in a converted
19th-century tenement building exudes
an almost southern German charm.
The hotel is located in a tree-lined
street, so the rooms are quiet, even
though it's just a couple of blocks from
the nightlife around Kollwitzplatz.

Hotelschiff Eastern Comfort

Mühlenstrasse 73–7; tel: 030-6676
3806; www.eastern-comfort.com;
U | S: Warschauer Strasse; €-€€
This quirky Friedrichshain hotel is
situated on a houseboat that has been
lovingly restored by captain and owner
Edgar von Schmidt. There are three different kinds of rooms (the best are 'class
I', on the upper deck). Most of them
have a great view of the Warschauer
Brücke. Beware, though, that the hotel
is not ideal for guests afraid of creepy-
crawlies – inevitable by the river – and
is not such a good choice in winter.

**Above from far
left:** retro chic is
big in Berlin; the
pool at the Adlon.

Berlin offers an excellent range of upmarket, gourmet restaurants, ethnic eateries and traditional German restaurants. In very recent years, young, innovative chefs rediscovering local cuisine or creating daring crossover dishes have turned Berlin into Germany's leading gourmet city. Expect to see constant change and the juxtaposition of established and crazier alternative choices.

The majority of the city's elegant first-class restaurants are located in Mitte, around Friedrichstrasse, while the hipper places tend to be located in districts such as Scheunenviertel. Prenzlauer Berg, Kreuzberg and Schöneberg are good places to go for ethnic choices, as well as some hidden German gems. Charlottenburg, particularly the area around Savignyplatz, is where to go if you are looking for arty bistro-style restaurants.

Charlottenburg

12 Apostel
Bleibtreustrasse 49; tel: 030-312 1433; www.12-apostel.de; S: Savignyplatz; €€

Price guide for a two-course meal for one with a glass of house wine:

€€€€   over 60 euros
€€€   40–60 euros
€€   25–40 euros
€   below 25 euros

Pizza is the food to order in this upmarket and sociable Italian restaurant tucked away next to the S-Bahn tracks off Savignyplatz. A young, fashionable crowds packs together on benches in the beer garden, munching on huge ultra-thin pizzas that go by the names of the 12 Apostles. The ultimate 'sin' here is the Pizza 'Judas', with super-rich toppings.

Dressler Restaurant
Kurfürstendamm 207–8; tel: 030-883 3530; www.restaurant-dressler.de; U: Uhlandstrasse; €€

An old-time favourite on the Ku'-damm, the Art Deco, brasserie-style Dressler attracts mostly an older, pre-show crowd (there's a theatre next door). It's a great choice if you like light French fare or solid Berlin food. In winter, the oven-roasted goose with red and green cabbage has to be tried; in summer, pull up a chair outdoors and enjoy fried local pike-perch.

Engelbecken
Witzlebenstrasse 31; tel: 030-615 2810; www.engelbecken.de; U: Sophie-Charlotte-Platz; €€

A well-kept secret among the alternative, arty crowd in this secluded part of Charlottenburg, the Engelbecken close to the Lietzensee (lake) is a real delight. The simple but bright dining hall offers a great selection of heavy Bavarian, Austrian and other southern dishes such as game goulash with

'Knödel', or (in season) Berlin favourites such as white asparagus with Hollandaise sauce and potatoes. In summer, the outdoor tables are popular, so reserve in advance.

Francucci's Ristorante

Kurfürstendamm 90; tel: 030-323 3318; www.francucci.com; U: Adenauerplatz; €€

A Berlin fixture for more than two decades, Francucci's is a laid-back North Italian restaurant popular with up-market locals. The menu changes frequently, but the homemade pasta, the freshly made hot and cold salads (including barbecued octopus or rabbit) and the fish (Dorade) dishes are delicious. Tables outside in summer.

Kuchi Kant

Kantstrasse 30; tel: 030-3150 7815; kant.kuchi.de; S: Savignyplatz; €€

This top-notch yet casual minimalist restaurant is always solidly booked for its freshly made sushi and Asian hot dishes such as Yaki-tori barbecue skewers, and for the friendly service. Take-away available next door.

Mar y Sol

Savignyplatz 5; tel: 030-313 2593; www.marysol-berlin.de; S: Savigny-platz; €€

With its tiled, ivy-covered terrace set around an attractive water fountain, this Spanish restaurant is a delightful place to hang out in summer. There's a huge selection of tapas, including dishes such as freshly fried sardines or spicy octopus, honey-glazed chicken pieces and meatballs in tomato sauce. Reserve in summer.

Paris Bar

Kantstrasse 152; tel: 030-313 8052; www.parisbar.net; U: Uhlandstrasse, S: Savignyplatz; €€

The ups and downs of the Paris Bar, Western Berlin's oldest 'in' place, where the Berlinale film stars and top artists used to rub shoulders, are still followed closely by a loyal clientele. The restaurant offers classic French food, but most guests come here for the wine selection and the flamboyant atmosphere of a worn-out but proud and likeable legend.

Scheunenviertel

Alpenstück

Gartenstrasse 9; tel: 030-2175 1646; www.alpenstueck.de; S: Nordbahnhof; €€

Leading a new trend in Berlin's ultra-hip restaurants, the Alpenstück offers a long-forgotten, highly calorific traditional German menu. Bavarian game and fish dishes, hearty German pasta and 'Knödel' or cabbage dishes are the order of the day here, as are the fresh beers and top-quality wines.

Monsieur Vuong

Alte Schönhauser Strasse 46; tel: 030-9929 6924; www.monsieur vuong.de; U: Weinmeisterstrasse; €

Above from far left: haute cuisine; hearty German dish, served with a ubiquitous gherkin; set for dinner.

Public Transport Note that in the practical information for each entry we quote the nearest U-Bahn (U) or S-Bahn (S) station.

This tiny, buzzing but soothing Vietnamese eatery is no longer an insider's secret, but the food remains delicious. The small daily selection of very fresh meat and great vegetarian dishes (with an emphasis on creations from the Mekong Delta) is complemented by friendly service and great teas.

Shiro i Shiro

Rosa-Luxemburg-Strasse 11; tel: 030-9700 4790; www.shiroishiro.com; U+S: Alexanderplatz; €€

At one time considered to be one of Berlin's top Japanese restaurants, the Shiro i Shiro lost some of its appeal, but is fortunately regaining its status as one of the hippest restaurants in Mitte thanks to the creatively composed sushi, the excellent hot Japanese dishes and the stylish all-white interior.

Friedrichstrasse

Aigner Gendarmenmarkt

Französische Strasse 25; tel: 030-2037 51850; www.aigner-gendarmenmarkt.de; U: Französische Str, S: Unter den Linden; €€€

The large yet cosy Austrian Aigner Gendarmenmarkt was brought to Berlin lock, stock and barrel to create the authentic flair of an old-style but elegant Vienese restaurant. The changing menu has some classics such as 'Tafelspitz' (boiled beef with horseradish) and Wiener schnitzel with excellent, just slightly warmed, potato salad. Rich sweets too.

Bocca di Bacco

Friedrichstrasse 167–8; tel: 030-2067 2828; www.boccadibacco.de; U: Französische Strasse; €€€€

This restaurant's Western cousin, the 'old' Bocca, as it's locally known, may be the real deal, but when in Mitte, the star-studded Bocca di Bacco is a great choice for artistic Italian food. The star factor here is high – it's popular with Hollywood stars in Berlin – so reservations and stylish attire are *de rigueur*.

Fischer's Fritz at The Regent

Charlottenstrasse 49; tel: 030-2033 6363; www.fischersfritzberlin.com; U: Französische Strasse; €€€€

The elegant Michelin-starred Fischer's Fritz, run by Christian Lohse (formerly at The Dorchester), is Berlin's top seafood restaurant. The varied menu changes regularly. The three-course lunch menus are good deals.

Grill Royal

Friedrichstrasse 105b; tel: 030-2887 9288; www.grillroyal.com; U+S: Friedrichstrasse; €€€

Beef is king in this stylish barbecue and grill restaurant, which is popular with the beautiful crowd and always fully booked. Expect top-quality meat, a great wine selection and a lively ambience.

San Nicci

Friedrichstrasse 101; tel: 030-3064 54980; www.san-nicci.de; U+S: Friedrichstrasse; €€€

Despite being owned by the highly regarded Roland Mary of the Borchardt *(see p.70)*, San Nicci got off to a bad start when it first opened, but has managed to turn things around to become quite a likeable modern Italian restaurant. Nestled in the Admiralspalast entertainment complex *(see p.69 and 118)*, it is the perfect pre-theatre spot (reservations strongly advised).

Vau

Jägerstrasse 54–5; tel: 030-202 9730; www.vau-berlin.de; U: Stadtmitte or Hausvogteiplatz; €€€€

The Vau was one of Berlin's first restaurants to receive Michelin stars after the fall of the Wall and remains a favourite. The stylish, minimalist interior, the artfully presented, light international food by chef Kolja Kleeberg and the friendly service make it a great and casual place to enjoy superb food.

Kreuzberg and Schöneberg

Altes Zollhaus

Carl-Herz-Ufer 30; tel: 030-691 7676; www.altes-zollhaus-berlin.de; U: Prinzenstrasse; €€

It's quite a surprise to find this rural building – located in an old customs house – in the heart of Kreuzberg. But the traditional restaurant, run since 1989 by Herbert Beltle, is one of the district's upmarket favourites. Highlights include delicious hearty oven-roasted country duck with savoy cabbage and potato cookies.

Le Cochon Bourgeois

Fichtestrasse 24; tel: 030-693 0101; www.lechochon.de; U: Südstern; €€

This cosy little restaurant is a must for Francophiles. Tucked away in the heart of Kreuzberg 61, the upscale Cochon serves some of the city's most traditional French fare such as veal sweetbreads or marinated veal head, accompanied with delicious wines.

Prenzlauer Berg

Mao Thai

Wörther Strasse 30; tel: 030-441 9261; www.maothai.de; U: Senefelder Platz, €€

One of Berlin's most traditional and upmarket Thai restaurants, Mao Thai serves delicious curries and seafood. Most of the dishes are rather mild, so ask the waiter to spice things up if you prefer hotter food.

Friedrichshain

Schneeweiss

Simplonstrasse 16; tel: 030-2904 9704; www.schneeweiss-berlin.de; U+S: Warschauer Strasse; €€

This stylish restaurant looks like a rather peculiar mix of a German canteen and a 21st-century lounge. The chef serves an ironic interpretation of heavy, old-style Alpine dishes such as the ubiquitous Wiener schnitzel and cheesy 'Spätzle' (delicious pasta noodles), and a daily changing lunch and dinner menu offering items including pork knuckle and fish dishes.

Above from far left: table set at the restaurant in the Brecht Haus, Chausseestrasse 125, tel: 030-282 3843; daily from 6pm; the historic Café Einstein on Kurfürstendamm (see p.55 for a review of Café Einstein on Unter den Linden).

In recent years, Berlin has gained a reputation for having one of the most diverse and vibrant nightlife scenes in Europe. Most of the action can be found in Mitte, Scheunenviertel and Spandauer Vorstadt (primarily around Oranienburger Strasse and Hackescher Markt). Kreuzberg, Prenzlauer Berg (around Kollwitzplatz) and Friedrichshain (around Boxhagener Platz) are good for non-mainstream venues. Further west, Charlottenburg's Ludwigkirchplatz and Savignyplatz are popular nightlife hubs. The select listings below start with more traditional venues for theatre, dance and classical music, before leading into clubs and bars. Information on a number of the city's arenas is also included here.

Note that at the end of the practical information for each entry we quote the nearest U-Bahn (U) or S-Bahn (S) station. Public transport in Berlin is excellent – at the weekends both U and S lines have an all-night service.

Theatre and Music

Admiralspalast

Friedrichstrasse 101; tel: 030- 4799 7499; www.admiralspalast.de; ticket office: 11am–7pm; U: Friedrichstrasse

The historic 'Operettentheater' has been beautifully restored and converted into the Admiralspalast entertainment complex. The main stage – the largest in Berlin – usually shows touring productions, from musicals to live-music acts to stand-up comedy (in German). *See also p.69.*

Bar Jeder Vernunft

Schaperstrasse 24; tel: 030-883 1582; www.bar-jeder-vernunft.de; ticket hotline: Mon–Sat noon–7pm, Sun 3–7pm; U: Spichernstrasse, Kurfürstendamm

One is of the city's leading comedy and cabaret places, set inside a 1920s tent, this venue has made the careers of top local acts including the Geschwister Pfister, Tim Fischer and Desirée Nick. Now presents an unorthodox mix of comedy and song. Note that it's difficult to enjoy unless you speak good German.

Deutsche Oper

Bismarckstrasse 35; tel: 030-3438 4343; www.deutscheoperberlin.de; ticket office: Mon–Sat from 11am; U: Bismarckstrasse

Originally built in 1912, destroyed in World War II and not rebuilt until 1961, the Deutsche Oper may not be as flashy at its Eastern counterpart, the Staatsoper *(see p.55 and 120)* but is well regarded for its innovative interpretations of classic works and for hosting internationally renowned performers.

English Theatre

Fidicinstrasse 40; tel: 030-691 1211; www.etberlin.de; ticket office: daily from 7pm; U: Platz der Luftbrücke

Berlin's only English-language theatre has a solid reputation for its perform-

ances that include American and British classics and new works.

Friedrichstadtpalast

Friedrichstrasse 107; tel: 030-2326 2326; www.friedrichstadtpalast.de; ticket office: Mon 10am–6pm, Tue–Sat 10am–6.30pm, Sun 10am–6pm; U+S: Friedrichstrasse

The 1970s façade of the Friedrichstadtpalast may be rather ugly, but the attractions inside don't disappoint. This is Europe's largest variety theatre, staging sumptuous shows with glamorous showgirls and high-flying acrobats that would give Las Vegas shows a run for their money. *See also p.69.*

Hebbel-Theater

Hau 1: Stresemannstrasse 29; Hau 2: Hallesches Ufer 32; Hau 3: Tempelhofer Ufer 10; tel: 030-2590 0427; www.hebbel-am-ufer.de; ticket office: daily noon–7pm; U: Möckernbrücke

This ensemble of three theatres in close proximity to each other provides a venue for contemporary German and international theatre, dance and performance art.

Komische Oper

Behrenstrasse 55–7; tel: 030 4799 7400; www.komische-oper-berlin.de; ticket hotline: Mon–Sat 9am–8pm, Sun 2–8pm; U: Französische Strasse

Berlin's smallest opera house, the 'Comic Opera' has built its reputation on daring productions by director Hans Neuenfels. Everything here is sung in German. *See also p.54.*

Musical Theater am Potsdamer Platz

Marlene-Dietrich-Platz 1; tel: 0180-544 44; www.stage-entertainment.de; ticket hotline: Mon–Fri 8am–8pm, Sat 8am–8pm, Sun 10am–8pm; U+S: Potsdamer Platz

Berlin's leading stage for musicals is a huge, modern theatre (doubling as main screening theatre during the Berlinale film festival), showing popular hits such as *Beauty and the Beast.* Note that all musicals put on here are in German, even if the title is quoted in English.

Philharmonie und Kammermusiksaal

Herbert-von-Karajan-Strasse 1; tel: 030-2548 8999; www.berliner-philharmoniker.de; ticket hotline: daily 9am–6pm; U+S: Potsdamer Platz

The Berliner Philharmoniker (Berlin Philharmonic), under the direction of Sir Simon Rattle, is considered by many to be the best symphony orchestra in the world, and classical music lovers may want to plan their trip around their ability to purchase hard-to-get tickets. Even if attending a performance is impossible, the building itself is unique. Completed by Hans Scharoun in 1963, its walls seem to flow like the music that fills them. *See also p.47.*

Above from far left: dancing girls in pink and (in *Swan Lake*) cyclist swans at the Friedrichstadtspalast.

Staatsoper

Unter den Linden 7; tel: 030-2035 4555; www.staatsoper-berlin.org; ticket office: Mon–Sat 10am–8pm, Sun 2–8pm; S: Unter den Linden, U+S: Friedrichstrasse

Located in East Berlin during the Cold War, the country's main opera house is now one of the biggest attractions in the historic renovation of the palace area on Unter den Linden. Currently headed by pianist and conductor Daniel Barenboim, it has a repertoire focusing on classical opera and ballet, although outreach is also important, either through the staging of modern productions or by getting opera out onto the street with outdoor screenings. *See also p.55.*

Theater des Westens

Kantstrasse 12; tel: 030-319 030; www.theater-des-westens.de; ticket office: Mon–Fri noon–5.30pm, Sat–Sun 10.30am–5.30pm; U+S: Zoologischer Garten

One of the city's most beautiful historic theatres, the Theater des Westens counts Josephine Baker, Marlene Dietrich and Enrico Caruso among its past performers. It's now used mostly for touring productions of popular musicals.

Tipi am Kanzleramt

Grosse Queralle; tel: 0180-327 9358; www.tipi-am-kanzleramt.de; ticket office: Mon–Sat noon–6.30pm, Sun 3–5.30pm; S: Hauptbahnhof or Unter den Linden

The larger counterpart to the Bar Jeder Vernunft *(see p.118)* is also a stage within a tent, but puts on more commercial shows, typically music and comedy.

Varieté Chamäleon

Rosenthaler Strasse 40–1; tel: 030-400 0590; www.chamaeleonberlin. de; ticket office: Mon–Fri 10am–8.30pm, Sat 10.30am–10pm, Sun noon–7pm; S: Hackescher Markt

Set in the historic Hackesche Höfe, the Chamäleon is Berlin's alternative variety theatre, putting on an ironic, often cheeky, interpretation of traditional variety theatre. *See also p.65.*

Cinemas

Arsenal – Institut für Film und Videokunst e.V.

Potsdamer Strasse 2; tel: 030-2695 5100; www.arsenal-berlin.de; U+S: Potsdamer Platz

The Berlin Film Institute's official art-house cinema is set in the Filmmuseum *(see p.46)* in the Sony Center and mostly shows German or European films, including retrospectives and (sometimes long-forgotten) screen classics.

Cinestar IMAX 3D/CineStar Original im Sony Center

Potsdamer Strasse 4 and 5; tel: 0180-511 8811; www.cinestar.de; U+S: Potsdamer Platz

This eight-screen multiplex cinema in the Sony Center *(see p.46)* is the largest in Berlin for English-language

Above: the Sony Center by night.

films – mostly Hollywood blockbusters, but with some smaller-scale movies. A cocktail bar and American-style food kiosks make this a favourite with expats and tourists. Adjacent Potsdamer Strasse 5) is an Imax cinema.

Odeon Berlin

Hauptstrasse 116; tel: 030-7870 4019; www.odeon-kino.de; U: Innsbrucker Platz, S: Schöneberg

One of the few English-language-only cinemas, the Odeon attracts a loyal local clientele. The seats may be worn and the screening technology a far cry from that of a multiplex, but the off-mainstream films make this a great choice for arthouse buffs. Monday is 'Kinotag' (Cinema day), with tickets as low as €5.

Jazz Clubs

A-Trane

Bleibtreustrasse 1; tel: 030-313 2550; www.a-trane.de; daily 9pm–2am, Fri and Sat 9pm–late; S: Savignyplatz

This is Berlin's best and best-known jazz club, hosting local and international performers in an intimate atmosphere. Reserve seats online.

Quasimodo

Kantstrasse 12a; tel: 030-312 8086; www.quasimodo.de; café: Mon–Fri from 4.30pm, Sat–Sun from 11am, club from 9pm; S: Savignyplatz

A cellar bar with stage and dancefloor, Quasimodo is a Berlin institution that hosts live jazz, funk and soul, Latin,

blues and rock bands. Check listings and get there early for good seats.

Arenas

O2 World Arena

O2 Platz 1; tel: 01803-206 070; www. o2world.de; ticket hotline: Mon– Fri 9am–9pm, Sat–Sun 10am–6pm; U+S: Warschauer Strasse, S: Ostbahnhof

This huge entertainment complex, opened in 2008 by American investor Philip Anschutz, reflects the ongoing urban regeneration of the Friedrichshain area *(see p.88)*. It stages a range of large-scale events, from sport (icehockey and the like) to pop music concerts and more.

Olympiastadion Berlin

Olympischer Platz 3; tel: 030-3068 8100; www.olympiastadion-berlin.de; tours daily 8am–4pm; U+S: Olympiastadion

The modernised 'five-star arena' not only hosts games played by Berlin's football team Hertha, but also the track-and-field event DKB-ISTAF and two or three major pop acts per year. Tours of the 1936 Olympic Stadium are also available.

Tempodrom

Möckernstrasse 10; tel: 030-747 370; www.tempodrom.de; ticket office: Mon–Fri noon–6.30pm, Sat 11am–7pm; U+S: Anhalter Bahnhof

This well-established fixture on the Kreuzberg scene stages popular live acts

as well as more off-mainstream World Music events and parties. It's housed in a white tent-like structure on the wide open area behind the ruins of the Anhalter Bahnhof *(see p.77)*.

Waldbühne

Am Glockenturm 1; tel: 030-9799 4811; www.ticketline-berlin.de; ticket hotline: Mon–Fri 10am–7pm, Sat 10am–1pm; U: Olympiastadion, S: Pichelsberg

With a capacity of 20,000, the Waldbühne, located close to the Olympic Stadium *(see p.121)*, is one of Europe's largest open-air amphitheatres and a great place to enjoy a summer night out in Berlin. It puts on open-air movies, popular music live acts and – generally regarded as the highlight of the season – one or two open-air concerts by the highly acclaimed Berlin Philharmonic Orchestra.

40 seconds

Potsdamer Strasse 58; tel: 030-8906 4241; http://40seconds.de; Fri, Sat 11pm–late; U+S: Potsdamer Platz

One of Berlin's top clubs, this ultra-cool but friendly place with great views of the skyline plays club, funk and soul music. Attracts a late-20s to mid-30s crowd.

Clärchens Ballhaus

Auguststrasse 24; tel: 030-282 9295; www.ballhaus.de; daily noon–late; S: Oranienburger Strasse

Berlin's last traditional 'Ballhaus' (ballroom), this place is ideal if you're looking for a little bit of nostaglia. The dancing here is mostly of the traditional type, such as salsa, tango, swing, cha-cha-cha and ballroom. Also holds special concerts on Sundays and a range of dance courses.

Felix

Behrenstrasse 73; Mon–Sat 8pm–late; www.felixrestaurant.de; S: Unter den Linden

This hip 1940s-style club in Mitte combines a restaurant, bar, lounge and club and pulls in a beautiful crowd. The music is usually house and soul. It holds themed nights, which are popular – expect long queues. Dress very smart and look your most gorgeous to get in.

SO 36

Oranienstrasse 190; www.so36.de; U: Kottbusser Tor

One of Kreuzberg's longest-running centres, SO 36 is popular with the gay community and the local crowd of partygoing students. Theme nights ring the changes.

Bar am Lützowplatz

Lützowplatz 7; tel: 030- 262 6807; www.baramluetzowplatz.de; daily 5pm–4am; U: Nollendorfplatz

An established fixture on the Berlin nightlife scene, this stylish place has the city's longest bar, where some of the

best drinks in town are poured by efficient, friendly staff. Attracts a stylish, well-to-do mid-20s to 30s crowd.

Bundespressestrand

Kapelle-Ufer 1; tel: 030-2809 9119; www.derbundespressestrand.de; late Apr–end of summer: daily 10am–late; S: Hauptbahnhof

Berlin's main beach bar on the banks of the River Spree is a great choice in summer and has great views of the Government district. Sip your cocktails under the stars or in one of the comfortable, covered lounge/bar areas.

Diener

Grolmanstrasse 47; tel: 030-881 5329; daily 6pm–3am; S: Savignyplatz

One of the most traditional 'Kneipen' (pubs) in Berlin, the no-nonsense Diener is famous for its cheeky service and great beer and wine. The clientele is mostly local actors and old-time regulars, with few tourists.

Green Door

Winterfeldtstrasse 50; tel: 030-215 2515; www.greendoor.de; Sun–Thur 6pm–3am, Fri–Sat 6pm–4am; U: Nollendorfplatz

The staff at this unpretentious 1960s retro-style bar mix some of the city's most delicious cocktails for a loyal clientele who are more interested in the drinks than in posing. You have to ring to be let in, but the door policy is usually fairly relaxed. A hidden gem.

Kumpelnest 3000

Lützowstrasse 23; tel: 030-261 6918; www.kumpelnest3000.com; daily 7pm–late; U: Kurfürstenstrasse

Set in a former brothel, Kumpelnest 3000 is dubbed Berlin's most famous 'Absackerkneipe' – a place you'd go for your last drink of the night. It's usually packed with an eclectic crowd, from local students to hip bohemian 30-somethings.

Vox Bar

Marlene-Dietrich-Platz 2; tel: 030-2553 1772; www.vox-restaurant. de/bar; daily 6pm–late; U+S: Potsdamer Platz

The fashionable minimalist bar in the Grand Hyatt *(see p.23 and 111)* offers live jazz and stylish pop music acts on a nightly basis. Renowned for its huge and outstanding whisky selection.

Watergate

Falckensteinstrasse 49a; Wed from 11pm, Fri and Sat from midnight; www.water-gate.de; U+S: Warschauer Strasse

Claiming to be one of top clubs in the world, the Watergate attracts top international DJs, who play techno and house music on its two dancefloors. In summer, the terrace gives extra floorspace for partying. The club has great views across the river to the elaborate 1896 Oberbaumbrücke, which links Kreuzberg with Friedrichshain and is beautifully illuminated at night.

Above from far left: at the Varieté Chamäleon *(see p.120);* on the city's Berlin famed clubbing scene.

CREDITS

Insight Step by Step Berlin
Written by: Jürgen Scheunemann
Series Editor: Clare Peel
Cartography Editors: Zoë Goodwin
and James Macdonald
Picture Manager: Steven Lawrence
Photography: All Pictures © APA/Jon Santa
Cruz except: AKG London 48TL; APA/Glyn
Genin 10, 11, 16, 74, 75; APA/Tony Halliday
30TR, 49TR, 53B; Berlin Tourism 22; Corbis 85,
122, 123; Everynight Images 22B; Jon Arnold
47T; Pictures Colour Library 54–5; iStockphoto
2–3, 2ML, 2BR, 6ML, 7TR, 7MR, 10TL, 10TR,
11B, 12, 13, 15TL, 15B, 23T, 29R, 31TR, 32, 33,
45, 48–9, 50–1, 56, 57, 62B, 71T, 71B, 92L, 92–3,
109; Leonardo 111; Robert Harding 86B; Stephan
Gustavus 118, 119; TIPS Images 120–1; Monika
Rittershaus/Lebrecht 55. **Front cover:** main
image: Corbis; BL left: Alamy; BR: iStockphoto.
Inside back cover map: Berlin Verkehrsbetriebe.
Printed by: Insight Print Services (Pte) Ltd,
38 Joo Koon Road, Singapore 628990

DISTRIBUTION

Worldwide
**APA Publications GmbH & Co. Verlag KG
(Singapore branch)**
38 Joo Koon Road
Singapore 628990
Tel: (65) 6865 1600
Fax: (65) 6861 6438

UK and Ireland
GeoCenter International Ltd
Meridian House, Churchill Way West
Basingstoke, Hampshire, RG21 6YR
Tel: (44) 01256 817 987
Fax: (44) 01256 817 988

United States
Langenscheidt Publishers, Inc.
36–36 33rd Street, 4th Floor
Long Island City, NY 11106
Tel: (1) 718 784 0055
Fax: (1) 718 784 0640

Australia
Universal Publishers
1 Waterloo Road, Macquarie Park, NSW 2113
Tel: (61) 2 9857 3700
Fax: (61) 2 9888 9074

New Zealand
Hema Maps New Zealand Ltd (HNZ)
Unit 2, 10 Cryers Road
East Tamaki, Auckland 2013
Tel: (64) 9 273 6459
Fax: (64) 9 273 6479

CONTACTING THE EDITORS

We would appreciate it if readers would alert us
to errors or outdated information by writing to
us at insight@apaguide.co.uk or APA Publications,
PO Box 7910, London SE1 1WE, UK.

www.insightguides.com

INDEX

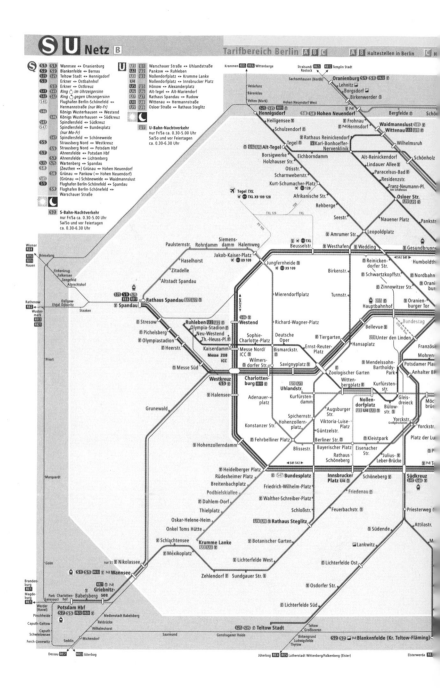